NICHO

Nicholas Wright's plays include *Vincent in Brixton* (Olivier Award for Best New Play 2003) and *Mrs Klein*, both at the National Theatre, in the West End and in New York; *Treetops* and *One Fine Day* at Riverside Studios; *The Gorky Brigade* at the Royal Court; *The Crimes of Vautrin* for Joint Stock; *The Custom of the Country* and *The Desert Air* for the RSC and *Cressida* for the Almeida. Adaptations: *His Dark Materials*, *Three Sisters* and *John Gabriel Borkman* for the National; *Thérèse Raquin* at Chichester Festival Theatre and the National; and *Naked* and *Lulu* at the Almeida. Screenplays include adaptations of novels by Patrick Hamilton, Doris Lessing, Josef Skvorecky, Armistead Maupin and Ford Madox Ford. He wrote the libretto for Rachel Portman's opera *The Little Prince* (Houston Grand Opera) and for Jonathan Dove's opera for television, *Man on the Moon*, based on the Apollo 11 moon landing. His writing about the theatre includes *99 Plays*, a personal review of playwriting from Aeschylus to the present day and *Changing Stages: A View of British Theatre in the Twentieth Century*, co-written with Richard Eyre.

Other titles in this series

Howard Brenton
BERLIN BERTIE
FAUST – PARTS ONE & TWO
  after Goethe
IN EXTREMIS
PAUL

Caryl Churchill
BLUE HEART
CHURCHILL PLAYS: THREE
CHURCHILL: SHORTS
CLOUD NINE
A DREAM PLAY *after* Strindberg
DRUNK ENOUGH TO SAY
  I LOVE YOU?
FAR AWAY
HOTEL
ICECREAM
LIGHT SHINING IN
  BUCKINGHAMSHIRE
MAD FOREST
A NUMBER
THE SKRIKER
THIS IS A CHAIR
THYESTES *after* Seneca
TRAPS

Ariel Dorfman
DEATH AND THE MAIDEN
PURGATORIO
READER
THE RESISTANCE TRILOGY
WIDOWS

David Edgar
ALBERT SPEER
CONTINENTAL DIVIDE
EDGAR: SHORTS
PENTECOST
PLAYING WITH FIRE
THE PRISONER'S DILEMMA
THE SHAPE OF THE TABLE

Kevin Elyot
THE DAY I STOOD STILL
ELYOT: FOUR PLAYS
FORTY WINKS
MOUTH TO MOUTH
MY NIGHT WITH REG

Debbie Tucker Green
BORN BAD
DIRTY BUTTERFLY
STONING MARY
TRADE & GENERATIONS

Edward Kemp
5/11
NATHAN THE WISE *after* Lessing

Tony Kushner
ANGELS IN AMERICA –
  PARTS ONE & TWO
CAROLINE, OR CHANGE
HOMEBODY/KABUL

Owen McCafferty
CLOSING TIME
DAYS OF WINE AND ROSES
  after JP Miller
MOJO MICKYBO
SCENES FROM THE BIG
  PICTURE
SHOOT THE CROW

Conor McPherson
DUBLIN CAROL
McPHERSON: FOUR PLAYS
McPHERSON PLAYS: TWO
PORT AUTHORITY
THE SEAFARER
SHINING CITY
THE WEIR

Arthur Miller
AN ENEMY OF THE PEOPLE
  after Ibsen
PLAYING FOR TIME

Enda Walsh
BEDBOUND & MISTERMAN
DISCO PIGS
  & SUCKING DUBLIN
THE SMALL THINGS

Nicholas Wright
CRESSIDA
HIS DARK MATERIALS
  after Pullman
MRS KLEIN
THERESE RAQUIN *after* Zola
VINCENT IN BRIXTON
WRIGHT: FIVE PLAYS

Nicholas Wright

THE REPORTER

introduced by the author

NICK HERN BOOKS

London

www.nickhernbooks.co.uk

A Nick Hern Book

The Reporter first published in Great Britain as a paperback original in 2007 by Nick Hern Books Limited, 14 Larden Road, London W3 7ST

Cover image: Peter King/Hulton Archive/Getty Images
Cover design by Ned Hoste, 2H

Typeset by Country Setting, Kingsdown, Kent CT14 8ES
Printed in Great Britain by Bookmarque, Croydon, Surrey

A CIP catalogue record for this book is available from the British Library

ISBN   978 1 85459 963 6

Introduction

'You have to remember that, with the possible exception of Robert Kee, Jim was the best of us all.' This was said to me by a fellow reporter of James Mossman's from the 1960s. We were talking in early 2005, a time when the culture of lies was so all-enveloping that even those who questioned it seemed to be somehow imprisoned inside its terms of reference. 'The aims of the occupation may be admirable . . . but is it working?' Watching the news, I longed for Mossman's ghost to appear on screen. His gift had always been to examine untruth without the slightest hint of fellow-feeling for it.

I saw him first on television in the early sixties. Viewers in those days had the choice of a mere two television channels and *Panorama* regularly went out to an audience of ten million. Mossman was handsome, rangy, brilliant. Weaving his way through a Hong Kong riot, chatting with Yemeni warlords or hitting the Vietnam trail with a company of US marines, he seemed partly reporter, partly some dazzlingly gifted proconsul sorting out a troublesome outpost of the Empire. Around this time, when I was working in a bookshop, he appeared at the counter and asked with a kind of searching diffidence if we had a copy of James Michie's translation of Horace's *Odes*. (We didn't.) A little later I used to pass him in the corridors of the BBC, where I was working as a Floor Assistant: this was basically the job of call-boy, assigned at random to whatever programme came up on the rota. A lazy day meant a long-running old warhorse like *Fanny Cradock* or *Jackanory*, when everyone concerned knew the routine so well that the Floor Manager would send me home. A good day meant a Ken Loach drama. An adrenalin-packed day meant Ned Sherrin's late-night satire programme, in which the running order was quite often thrown up in the air while the show was going out live. Mossman was an occasional guest on Ned's panel discussions: an intense, incisive figure standing out starkly among the professional humorists. I saw him just once after this, one early evening in the Opera Tavern across the street from Drury Lane. He was with his lover Louis, whom I had known some years before. It was the night of the American-inspired coup that toppled the Diem regime in South Vietnam. Overawed, I made a stupid remark about it. Mossman was taut and angry about the day's events, and clearly thought I was an idiot. But he took the trouble to put me straight. I've reconstructed some of what he said, as well as I can remember it, in the play.

Once, when I was Floor Assisting on either *Panorama* or its rival programme *Tonight* – I forget which – Richard Dimbleby, the nation's senior broadcaster, who was scheduled to anchor the programme, was unexpectedly absent. There were whispered conversations among the studio top brass and an air of drama. Robin Day arrived amid much self-generated fuss and stood in as anchor. The Floor Manager, Joan Marsden – one of those forceful, loyal BBC people who gave a heart to the Corporation – was visibly upset, but took care to conceal what she knew. This scene came back to me vividly forty years later.

So did the studio interview with Harold Wilson, which by chance I saw live on air, that first sent Mossman's television career spinning off-track. It angered even Hugh Carleton Greene, the BBC's famously liberal Director-General. Mossman 'had shown too much personal emotion,' he stated at the next News and Current Affairs meeting. 'He had not been justified in appearing personally involved.' In a later interview with Commonwealth leaders, Mossman focused harshly on the Prime Minister of Singapore's habit of throwing his political opponents into prison. Greene circulated a furious memo: 'Mossman's handling of the discussion last night was absolutely deplorable . . . He was opinionated and rude . . . Has the time come when we should decide once and for all that Mossman should not be used any more in roles to which he is unsuited?'

The management discussions that followed are portrayed in the minutes, in normal BBC fashion, as taking place entirely between acronyms, albeit ones with quite distinct personalities. HCAG Tel defended Mossman stoutly, pointing out that most of the Commonwealth ministers concerned 'had stayed on afterwards in the best of humour.' ENCA tried a calming

approach: 'Mossman's frustration at receiving evasive replies to
his questions was understandable, but his tone had been wrong.'
But MD Tel was taking no prisoners: 'Mossman's offensiveness,
on this as on previous occasions, had stemmed from his self-
righteousness.' He was 'impervious to ordinary reprimands, and
the point could be best be made by . . . declining to use him as
interviewer/chairman unless absolutely necessary.' HCAG Tel
counter-attacked with the ingenious argument that 'excluding
him from interviews and discussions would make his other
services proportionally more expensive.' But for DG Designate
(the incoming Director-General, Greene being on his way out)
decorum came first. It was, he judged, 'unfair to the BBC and to
Mossman to put him in a role for which he was not fitted, even
if the cost of not doing so was high.'

Greene and the acronyms were presiding over a revolution that
they couldn't control. Only a few years before, political interviewers had been politely deferential. 'Would you care, Home
Secretary, to enlarge on the statement that you made to the
House of Commons this afternoon?' By the late sixties deference
seemed absurd. But how far could an interviewer go in the
direction of disrespect? How far could television itself evolve
from a realm of enlightenment, innocent fun and life-as-it-
ought-to-be into a confrontational rough-house loud with the
noise of life-as-it-is? Nobody knew. Mossman stood precisely at
this cusp of change, though the abyss of darkness and
uncertainty that he saw before him had a subjective aspect too.

I spoke with a number of people who had worked, like him, in
current affairs. Seldom have I met such a wise and informative
lot. Not one banged on about the golden age when a team of as
few as two, never more than four, in some unfamiliar place of
crisis, devoid of any precise editorial brief, could make a first-
class piece of documentary purely by following their instincts.
Yet they evoked that age, and I kept thinking: how bold it was,
how well it worked.

I talked with many other of Mossman's friends and colleagues.
Everyone remembered him with the greatest clarity, because he
had made such a sharp impression at the time. I sometimes felt
that I was tapping a memory-well that had been kept fresh for
just this purpose.

Their memories were inconsistent with each other, as you would
expect of such a compartmentalised life. Many described his
passion for the truth, but he also emerged as a raconteur whose
stories were packed with exaggerations. Straight colleagues
remembered his implacable seriousness; gay friends who shared
his social life remembered his frivolous wit, not all of which
travels well. ('His Lady Bracknell imitation was hilarious.') A
woman who had known him since his undergraduate days spoke
movingly of their love for each other when young. To a respected
senior at the BBC, he was a true professional: 'You could send
him anywhere and say you wanted twelve minutes, and that's
what you got.' Others described him turning a deaf ear to orders
that didn't suit him. His rudeness to people he didn't like got a
couple of mentions, and so did his kindness to those he did. The
young researchers on his final Arts programme, some of them
now eminent in television, couldn't speak highly enough of the
thoughtful way in which he had brought them on.

His patrician manner turned out to be part-invention. His father,
a Royal Flying Corps pilot, had been killed in a plane crash before
he was born, after which he and his brother were brought up in a
small mews flat over a garage off Westbourne Grove from which
their beloved mother and equally beloved aunt went off each day
to work, respectively, in a bank and a toy factory in order to
send Jim and his brother to public school. There was talk of a
moneyed and grand connection but it remained remote. Jim's
attempts in later years to track down the family coat of arms got
nowhere at all. Characteristically, he saw the funny side of this.
'I met a horrid little man who told me that my family is *completely*
undistinguished!' he told a friend, shaking with laughter.

Other memories of him were darker. The crime of Vietnam was
a persistent shadow that he couldn't dispel. Foreign reporting had
burned him out . . . well, that's one theory. He was disillusioned
with television, he'd been reprimanded once too often, he was
in grief. One young researcher had remarked how pleasant it
was that spring had arrived. 'That means nothing to me at all,'
Jim replied, more puzzled than anything else, before adding,
awkwardly, 'I don't know why.'

The common factor across the board was a sense of distance.
'One could never get under the skin of him.' 'He was different

from the rest of us.' 'There was a shell that one couldn't penetrate.' Even close friends would interrupt the interview with the sudden remark: 'You know, I'm not sure that I really knew him at all.'

The shock at the news of his death was compounded when his interview with the philosopher Stuart Hampshire went out soon after. In steering the conversation on to the subject of unhappiness, this most private and secret of interviewers had finally revealed his inner self to the viewing public. In BBC Kensington House, where the programme had been edited, his team watched the film in amazement: 'Did Jim really *say* that?'

To anyone who knew him, the Jim of my play will be only a shadow of Jim in life. Relying on conflicting sources, and a little imagination, I have tried to create a shadow with more facets than he chose to reveal to any one person still alive. I owe great thanks to the many people who shared their recollections with me. And I was helped by a number of books, among them Peter Adam's memoir of a remarkable life both in and out of the BBC, *Not Drowning but Waving*, and Selina Hastings' biography of Rosamond Lehmann: it was here that I learned of the odd but somehow consummatory friendship between novelist and reporter.

The play is not a biography nor a history but a play. It follows the essential architecture of James Mossman's life and death, but many incidents have been changed, and others invented, for dramatic effect. As a general rule, the more unlikely events are the ones that really happened. Jim, Louis and Rosamond are depicted as themselves, as far as I am capable of doing so. The same is true of Robin Day and Joan Marsden. All other BBC personnel and the character of Marko are imaginary, and should not be confused with anyone living or dead.

Nicholas Wright

The Reporter was first performed in the Cottesloe auditorium of the National Theatre, London, on 21 February 2007 (previews from 14 February), with the following cast:

JAMES MOSSMAN	Ben Chaplin
MARKO	Aleksander Mikic
WAITERS	Angelo Paragoso
JOAN MARSDEN / MRS RUDGE	Tilly Tremayne
ROBIN DAY	Paul Ritter
RAY RAY	Bruce Alexander
CAMERAMAN	John Cummins
DANIEL	Leo Bill
LOUIS	Chris New
MOLLY	Gillian Raine
HAROLD WILSON	Patrick Brennan
ROSAMOND LEHMANN	Angela Thorne

Director   Richard Eyre
Designer   Rob Howell
Lighting Designer   Peter Mumford
Sound Designer   Rich Walsh
Video Designer   Jon Driscoll

THE REPORTER

2

Characters

JAMES MOSSMAN (JIM), *reporter*

MARKO, *cameraman*

JOAN MARSDEN, *floor manager*

ROBIN DAY, *reporter*

RAY RAY, *BBC executive*

DANIEL, *research assistant*

LOUIS, *potter*

MOLLY, *James's mother*

HAROLD WILSON, *Prime Minister*

ROSAMOND LEHMANN, *novelist*

MRS RUDGE, *clairvoyant*

BBC STAFF and CREW, a TEA LADY, WAITERS, etc.

The play is set in East Anglia, Saigon, London and San Francisco between 1963 and 1971.

This text went to press before the end of rehearsals so may differ slightly from the play as performed.

ACT ONE

Jim's House in Norfolk

1971. JIM *is forty-four.*

JIM (*as if to camera*). I'm standing in the living room of a
house in Norfolk. It's early spring. The fields are bleak with
promise. There's a wind blown in from the sea, a wind that
clatters the glazing and whistles down the chimneystack like
the protesting cry of some invisible victim.

The room has been knocked through from front to back like
a house in London. Stripped-pine floors, an Afghan kelim
rug, a sofa from Heals and not much else. White walls, on
which are a few good prints and an original painting by Keith
Vaughan of two boys playing football on a beach. A stone
Buddha from Laos keeps watch from the floor, a Sri Lankan
demon-mask hangs over the doorway, and a handmade spiral
staircase leads up to the bedrooms.

Here on a table is that item of long cliché, the reporter's
battered typewriter. Beside it, letters, notebooks, drafts. A
stoneware pot, handmade, in subdued colours. Finally, a note
in pencil.

(*He reads.*) 'I can't bear it any more, though I don't know
what "it" is.'

The 'it' is cradled inside a pair of inverted commas, as though
to protect the word against inquiry. But a reporter must
inquire. It's what we do. What is 'it'? How could a man in
whose death 'it' played such an intimate part, not know? The
search begins with a snapshot of the reporter's life. The year
is 1963, the place, Saigon, a city of colonial charm, seductive
boulevard life and jacaranda trees.

Saigon

JIM *sits at a café table. A* WAITER *is serving coffee and croissants.* MARKO *arrives. He has his Arriflex camera, a kitbag containing sound equipment, batteries, etc. and an airmail copy of a French newspaper. He's Bosnian, fit, extrovert.*

MARKO. Jim, hi!

He embraces JIM.

JIM. Morning.

MARKO. You look wiped out.

He sits.

(*To the* WAITER.) Café!

(*To* JIM.) It's beautiful day, huh? Hey, look at those two.

He follows two passing young women through the lens of his Arriflex. Murmurs:

Keep moving. That's good, that's good.

JIM. Yes, they're very pretty, Marko, but they're not what I'm here to film.

MARKO. Don't worry, we got some action. Tomorrow morning, Mekong Delta, two Vietnamese battalions of the 7th Division will make surprise attack on VC-held village.

JIM. How do you know?

MARKO. I know.

JIM. How far is it from Saigon?

MARKO. Sixty kilometres, Jim. That's all. And look around us! Fools' paradise!

JIM. Good, fine. We'll need to go to . . . (the press office).

MARKO. We don't do anything, Jim, it's all fixed up. I have good friend at the US Advisers' Mission. Major Dawkins. Terrible man, good soldier. He will fly us to scene of operation at O-five-hundred hours tomorrow.

JIM. Why?

MARKO. He owes me a favour, OK? Don't ask.

JIM. Well done.

The WAITER *arrives with coffee.*

MARKO. A pleasure. (*To the* WAITER.) *Hep, garçon! Ces croissants sont rassis! Remportez-les et apportez-en nous des frais!*

WAITER. *Désolé, monsieur! Je vous avais pris pour des Américains. Je vous en apporte des frais tout de suite.*

He takes the croissants away. JIM *takes out a book: Nabokov's* Pale Fire. MARKO *opens his French-language newspaper and reads. As if to camera:*

JIM. Few words inspire such foreboding in the heart of a travelling reporter as 'You'll have to pick up a local cameraman.' Marko was different. He caught what nobody else could see. The lie in the face of the smiling colonel. The pickpocket at work. The gun beneath the load on the buffalo-cart. How he got from Sarajevo to Saigon, I never found out.

MARKO *looks up from his newspaper.*

MARKO. This will interest you.

JIM. Mm hm?

MARKO. 'Master-spy Kim Philby has arrived in Moscow.'

JIM. Let me see.

He takes the newspaper and reads.

MARKO. Philby was double agent. MI6, KGB, yes?

JIM. So it seems.

MARKO. Did you know him?

JIM. Yes, I did, as a matter of fact. Only slightly.

MARKO. It says he disappeared in Beirut three months ago.

JIM. That sounds about right.

MARKO. You were filming in Beirut three months ago. You told me last night. Did you meet him there?

JIM. Yes, of course. Any reporter would have looked him up.
We had a drink in the bar of the St Georges. Then my
cameraman came down, and he and I went off and had
dinner. I'd no idea that Kim was working for the Russians.
As far as I was concerned, he was simply a boring old drunk
who happened to be stringing for the *Observer*.

MARKO. What did you say to each other?

JIM. Why do you ask?

MARKO. Because after I left you last night, I met American
guy who said two things about you. One was, you are fine
reporter.

JIM. What was the other?

MARKO. That you are British spook.

JIM *laughs*.

JIM. Well, if I were, and if Kim Philby knew that, I can assure
you that spying is the last thing we would have talked about.

He hands the paper back to MARKO. *Fresh croissants
arrive.*

(*As if to camera*.) My not-so-secret life as an operative in
MI6 began when my tutor at Cambridge steered me towards
an office near St James's Park, where I was interviewed by a
man who looked like the character actor Raymond Huntley.
That's when the travelling started. They got me excellent
covers: the *Telegraph*, the *Daily Mail*. I left the firm, as much
as anyone does, when I joined the BBC, on the grounds that I
couldn't inhabit two Kafka's castles at the same time. I
retained a highly trained ability to conceal. Or, as I sometimes
think, an inability not to. Could that be 'it'? No, spying never
drove anyone to suicide. To drink, yes.

The WAITER *is there*.

WAITER. *Votre taxi est arrivé, monsieur.*

JIM. I didn't order a taxi.

MARKO. I did. There is Buddhist procession starting at Central
Market. And there is local guy I know, who says we mustn't
miss out on this.

JIM. Why not?

MARKO. Jim, I don't know. But he is very good guy.

JIM. Very well. Let's go. (*As if to camera.*) In those days of
innocence, I used to record my voice-overs in hotel lavatories
with blankets over the window to deaden the traffic noise.
Then I'd pack up the film, the tapes, the cutting order, go out
to the airport, find a friendly pilot and send it to London like a
Christmas parcel. Days later a telex might arrive, laconic, brief:
'Your story transmitted, twelve minutes.' Very occasionally,
'Well done.' The only times that I saw the film myself, were
when I returned to London. Then I'd watch on a monitor in
Lime Grove Studios: a leaking hell-hole at the back of
Shepherd's Bush Green, tenaciously clung to over the years
on the grounds that outward luxury would be superfluous to a
department so superior to any other as BBC Current Affairs.

BBC Lime Grove Studios

Stairs lead up to the gallery. Panorama *is coming up for
transmission. The Floor Manager,* JOAN MARSDEN, *in her
forties, is on her radio-mike, speaking to the gallery.*

JOAN. Robin's on his way. I've called him twice.

JIM (*as if to camera*). Joan Marsden, Floor Manager, known as
'Mother'.

ROBIN DAY *appears, flanked by a diffident and ordinary-
looking young man. This is* DANIEL. ROBIN *clutches a
cyclostyled running order.*

ROBIN. I'm here, I'm here. I know my way!

He brushes DANIEL *aside.*

God help us, where do they find these people?

JIM (*as if to camera*). Robin Day, known to his rivals in the bar
as 'Cruel Glasses'.

ROBIN *sees* JOAN.

ROBIN. Mother, dear, will you tell somebody up there that I've had to leave the Chancellor of the Exchequer practically on his own in Hospitality, so he'll need some love and attention. I wouldn't mind some myself. All anyone's told me is that Richard's ill and that I've got to be anchor.

RAY RAY comes down from the gallery. Mid-fifties, conventional, discreetly military.

RAY RAY. I'm coming down. Hello, Robin. I'm so sorry to spring this on you . . .

JIM (*as if to camera*). Ray Ray, Dep. ETN Tel.

ROBIN. No trouble at all, I'm happy to stand in.

RAY RAY. It's just that . . .

ROBIN. Any time! Although a little more notice would be welcome. It's not, um, not too serious with Richard, is it? Not the same old trouble?

RAY RAY. I couldn't tell you. And the feeling is, that there's no need to make any reference to his health.

ROBIN. So we keep the viewers guessing?

RAY RAY. They won't start guessing, unless we give them something to guess about. Understood?

ROBIN. Absolutely. We mustn't indulge in the open candour that we demand of others. Have no fear. I'll be my normal, unflappable self and it'll all be fine.

RAY RAY. Thanks, Robin. I can't tell you how much I appreciate this.

He starts going back up to the gallery.

Is everything all right, Mother?

JOAN. Yes, thank you, Ray Ray.

ROBIN stares at the front of a camera in incredulity.

ROBIN. What's that doing there?

CAMERAMAN. What, that, Mr Day? It's a teleprompter.

ROBIN. Yes, I know what it is. Who asked for it?

CAMERAMAN. Not one of us, Mr Day. It was him.

He indicates DANIEL, *who steps forward embarrassed.*
ROBIN *addresses him fiercely.*

ROBIN. And why?

JIM (*as if to camera*). Robin's ferocious style of questioning
was apt to paralyse his victims.

DANIEL. I'm sorry . . . I er know that Richard Dimbleby
doesn't need one, but I thought that . . .

ROBIN. How kind. However, I have been addressing the nation
on a variety of topics for well over a decade without the
benefit of a teleprompter, so I don't need one either. Have it
removed.

DANIEL *moves to go.*

JOAN. Leave it, Daniel. Robin, it's got to stay, but it won't be
running.

ROBIN. Well, that beggars belief. Is Jim Mossman here?

JIM. Hello, Robin.

ROBIN. Ah, Jim! Welcome back to real life. We see you in
London all too seldom. I've not had a chance to watch your
film. I'm told it's remarkable. Vietnam is very important, is
it?

JIM. It will be.

ROBIN. Well, you would know. Forgive me if I raise a query.
Nothing personal.

He speaks up for the benefit of the gallery.

Hello? Hello? Is Ray Ray there? Is anyone there, or are we
running on autopilot?

JOAN. They can hear you, Robin.

Loudly, ROBIN *addresses the gallery.*

ROBIN. I see from my running order that Jim's Vietnam film is
seventeen minutes long. So which two of my ten questions to
the Chancellor do you want me to cut? Because there won't
be time for them all.

A CAMERAMAN *hands him a headset.* ROBIN *presses an earpiece against his ear.*

What? You can't be serious. That one's essential.

JOAN. Robin, we're about to go.

ROBIN. Forget it. I'll just have to cut the Chancellor short.

Approaching his place:

Mother, what's happening? Where's the anchorman's chair? No, not this office chair, I want the big one!

JOAN. I'm sorry, Robin, but that chair is Richard Dimbleby's chair, and I'm not having anyone else sitting in it till either Richard comes back, or we know where we are. All right?

ROBIN. Very well, I know my place.

He takes the proffered chair.

Jim, I'll see you in Hospitality. I have much to tell you. It's been a madhouse here, you couldn't invent it.

JOAN. Quiet in the studio! Clock running!

Silence. A camera approaches ROBIN. *The clock on the monitors counts down 10 to 1. The* Panorama *title runs as the theme tune plays. Green lights turn red.* JOAN *signals to* ROBIN.

ROBIN. Good evening. In *Panorama* tonight, I shall be asking the Chancellor of the Exchequer about Britain's prospects of joining the Common Market. Jim Mossman reports on the current situation in Vietnam. But first, Robert Kee investigates Britain's Polaris missile. Is it an essential factor in the Anglo-American alliance? Or merely overrated, overpriced and over here?

Film of Polaris runs on the monitors.

JIM (*as if to camera*). There will be seven deaths, each one a step on the journey towards that cryptic suicide note. This is the first. In the Central Market of Saigon, a procession gathers. There is no joy in it. Something's wrong. Monks are chanting prayers and chiming bells, but all with an air of sombre preoccupation. A battered grey sedan draws up and a monk climbs out, a plastic container in his hand. He takes a few steps, then sits cross-legged on a pavement, lithely, lissomly, though he is old. He tips the container over his head, takes out a cigarette lighter and clicks it. There's a tower of flame and a barbecue smell. Cameras are focused, light meters held up to the sky. For the next ten minutes, until he topples to the ground like a charcoal marionette, I see his face. Mask-like. Impenetrable.

In the studio: the transmission is over. JOAN *has just come in.* JIM *is alone.*

JOAN. Are you not going through to 'Hostility'?

JIM. No, I can't stand the bitching.

JOAN. Nor me. What's it like being back?

JIM. Not bad. Just rather quiet and a bit parochial. When the plane comes down at Heathrow, I always expect to see sheep grazing on the runway.

JOAN. You ought to use that. Where are you off to next?

JIM. Wherever they send me.

JOAN. Do you never get sick of it?

JIM. I am sick of it. I'm just a silly old tart who spends half my life in aeroplanes and the other half pronouncing about the sufferings of the world. What's the story about Richard?

JOAN. Do you want the story, or the truth?

JIM. The truth.

JOAN. It's bad.

JIM. I'm sorry.

Near tears, JOAN *busies herself with something else.*

JOAN. Yes, it's awful. I don't know how they'll manage without him. You boys are all very clever. More than Richard really, in an intellectual way. But you haven't the weight. Richard *is Panorama.*

JIM. 'The voice of the nation.'

JOAN. Are you being funny?

JIM. No.

JOAN. Don't be. Can I give you a lift?

JIM. Yes, that'd be nice.

JOAN. Is it still Ken High Street?

JIM. Next to the Odeon, yes.

JOAN. I'll drop you off.

JIM (*as if to camera*). A pair of goodnights cut short by the slam of a car door. Joan's Morris Minor vanishing into the dark. The glance over the road at an unlit window in a row of Regency houses, now split into two-room flats, almost all of which are occupied by homosexuals. The vision of what I will find in mine: an empty fridge and a stack of unopened letters. The swivelling turn, the semi-abstracted stroll, not over the road and home, but leftwards into the long, dark, leafy walk that runs up the side of Holland Park. The flutter of anticipation. The thrill of anonymity. The allure of strangers. This isn't 'it', by the way. It's just itself.

Holland Walk

JIM *sits on a bench*. LOUIS *approaches*. *Younger than* JIM, *slim, intense. He sits.*

LOUIS. Hi.

JIM *glances at him, nods coolly.*

JIM. Hello.

LOUIS. I saw you on the TV tonight.

JIM. I'm sorry, you must be thinking of someone else.

LOUIS *laughs.*

LOUIS. Don't you recognise me?

JIM. Should I?

LOUIS. Yeah, you should. You've seen me taking the garbage out. You live in Number 18, right? I'm in 16. Second floor.

JIM. Oh, with Keith?

LOUIS. That's right. You were meant to come to one of his chic little dinner parties, only you never showed up.

JIM. You're Louis?

LOUIS. Yep.

JIM. Louis the potter.

LOUIS. That's me.

JIM. American.

LOUIS. Canadian. There's a difference.

JIM. I know. How's Keith?

LOUIS. You mean, 'Where's Keith?'

JIM. All right, where's Keith?

LOUIS. He's conducting *Lulu* in Madrid.

JIM. I see.

LOUIS. No you don't. You think the cat's away, so the mice will play. We're not together. Not any more.

JIM. I see. I mean, I *do* see. Well, don't let me hold you up.

LOUIS. Why do you say that?

JIM. Because I don't suppose you're here in order to have polite conversations with the neighbours.

LOUIS. That's not what I'm doing. Is that what you're doing?

He grins in a friendly way.

Besides, I'm only a neighbour till the end of the week. Keith wants me out. He wants his eighteenth-century prints back up on the walls and his cute little ornaments in place and a new bathroom mirror. I guess you heard what happened to the old one?

JIM. No.

LOUIS. You missed a very exciting rumour. By the time it'd gone up and down the terrace and back to me again, Keith had required eight stitches and I'd been carried off in a straitjacket. Which is crap.

JIM. The stitches or the straitjacket?

LOUIS. Both. I'm not crazy. I'm the only person I know who's got a certificate to prove he's sane.

JIM looks at him with new interest. LOUIS rolls a cigarette with tobacco from a little ceramic pot. JIM notices it.

JIM. Did you make that?

LOUIS. Sure. You want a roll-up?

JIM. I'll have one of my own.

He takes out a Senior Service.

LOUIS. Wanna light?

JIM. Thanks.

LOUIS lights his cigarette.

LOUIS. Will you go back to Vietnam?

JIM. Over and over, I expect.

LOUIS. Why do you say that?

JIM. Because it won't go away.

LOUIS. Why not?

JIM. Because . . . are you interested?

LOUIS. Sure.

JIM. Well, it's a proxy war between the two great powers, and each of them thinks that, if they want to get out some day, they can draw a line across the middle of Vietnam and that'll be the end of it.

He looks at LOUIS.

What?

LOUIS. Go on.

JIM. But the Vietnamese don't give a fuck about the Cold War. They're fighting the same war of independence that they've been fighting for centuries, against the Chinese, then the

French, and now the Americans. So they won't give up.
They'll never give up. It will be an endless, bloody
conflagration, and the irony is that we Westerners can't get
this into our stupid heads.

LOUIS. Why didn't you say that tonight?

JIM. I say it next week. We filmed a military op, and it covers
all that.

LOUIS. Do they let you say what you like?

JIM. Yes, more or less. Some old fool wrote in a memo once,
'Your man Mossman has a regrettable habit of speaking his
mind, but he appears to have a halo of protection.' It won't
last, of course.

LOUIS. Then what?

JIM. Then I'll compère quizzes, or I'll write book reviews for
the *New Statesman*. Or I'll sit in a Bayswater bedsit reading
Trollope. Aren't you cold?

LOUIS. No.

JIM. What did you think of the film tonight?

LOUIS. I hated it.

JIM. Why?

LOUIS. You were good. You were outspoken. You were stern.
But, Jim, that monk was burning himself to death. He was
dying in agony, and there wasn't a moment when I felt the
horror of that.

JIM. That's what it's like. You film some hideous, gut-wrenching
event, and then you see it on screen and somehow, in the
course of the writing and the editing and all the million other
things . . . it's vanished. The images are there, the words are
there, but the reality's gone.

LOUIS. You should've been more involved. You should've
showed how you felt about it.

JIM. No, that's rubbish. If I'd been more involved, then I
wouldn't be doing my job.

LOUIS. Why not?

JIM. Because it wasn't my story. It was his. I was outside it. I had to stay outside, in order to report it. That's how it works.

LOUIS. Maybe. But wouldn't it be nice, just for once, if you said something so outrageous that your halo broke?

JIM (*as if to camera*). The following Saturday, he took me to the Lucy Rie exhibition at the Potters' Gallery. I watched him examining each pot, his face up close, alight with a kind of goofy pleasure. I thought, 'It's true. I've fallen in love.' That's when I knew the travelling had to stop. Was it also when 'it' became inevitable? My queer friends lined up to warn me off him. They scented danger. On the other hand, so did I.

LOUIS *glances around. Stands.*

(*To* LOUIS.) Will you come back for a cup of coffee?

LOUIS. Let's not be banal. It's too important for that. You doing anything Saturday?

JIM (*who is doing many things that day*). No.

LOUIS. Keep it free.

He walks away without looking back.

JIM. Goodnight.

LOUIS *has gone.*

(*As if to camera.*) Death Number Two is that of Richard Dimbleby, who died on the eve of Christmas 1965. His last big job had been the funeral of Winston Churchill: the end of an era, everyone called it, and they were right. But Richard gave the past so living a form that it seemed immortal. Britain, in all its bravery, tolerance, grandeur, had survived. Duty and privilege had survived. He made them glorious. No one else could have done it. No one else would have meant it.

Jim's Mother's Flat

It's over a mews garage off Westbourne Grove. MOLLY *is there with* JIM. *She's spirited, poor, middle class.*

MOLLY. Was he a nice man?

JIM. Richard? Well, he probably wasn't quite as nice as he seemed to the viewers, but then none of us is. He was incredible at his job.

MOLLY. Then why did they give him less and less to do?

JIM. He wasn't well. Besides, some of the editorial chaps thought he was a bit old-fashioned.

MOLLY. Patriotism *is* old-fashioned, isn't it? I think the sun's over the yardarm. Pour me a drink, my darling. You know how I like it.

JIM. 'Just pass the Martini bottle through a ray of sunlight.'

MOLLY. Exactly. Help yourself to your Glenfiddich. Nobody's touched it since I saw you last.

He mixes a gin Martini and pours a scotch. She lights a cigarette.

JIM. Oh, Mother, you're not still smoking?

MOLLY. It relaxes me. Mrs Dabrowska came round to see your programme. You remember her, don't you? She's practically the last of the old crowd to have her marbles in place. We watched together on the big new set you gave me. You've been so good to me. I don't know what I'd do without you.

JIM. I do have a brother.

MOLLY. Yes, but he's married. You're free.

JIM laughs ironically.

Why are you laughing?

JIM. No reason.

MOLLY. So you say. I'd give a lot to know what goes on inside that head of yours.

JIM. Well, what's inside it at the moment is something you'll be very interested to hear. I had a meeting yesterday with Ray Ray . . .

MOLLY. Who's Ray Ray?

JIM. I've told you. He's one of my bosses. I said that I want to give up foreign reporting for a while, and concentrate on studio work. Pieces to camera, and political interviews and punditry. And he was . . . Are you listening?

MOLLY. What's punditry?

JIM. It doesn't matter. What I'm trying to tell you, is that I'll be working in London from now on. No more six-month absences, with the occasional postcard from Bangkok . . .

MOLLY *gasps in horror.*

Now what is it?

MOLLY. Is it because of something that you and your brother are keeping from me?

JIM. What are you talking about?

MOLLY. If I'm dying, you've got to tell me.

JIM. Mother, you're not dying. You're not even ill. Look at you! It's all ridiculous self-indulgence. This isn't even *about* you.

MOLLY. So I'm all right?

JIM. Yes.

MOLLY. And you haven't been sacked?

JIM. No!

MOLLY. Because you don't have a pension.

JIM. Yes, I know that!

She cries.

Don't cry.

MOLLY. I think about dying all the time. I've been going round putting stickers under all the family things saying, 'This is for Jimmy', and 'This is for John'.

JIM. You're absurd.

MOLLY. I know.

JIM. How's your Martini?

She sips it.

MOLLY. Perfect.

He looks at his watch.

I saw that!

JIM. I can't stay long. I've got some people to meet. I'm having the flat redone.

MOLLY. Who'll choose the colours?

JIM. There won't be colours. It's all going to be very stark and simple. I've found a young artist who's going to advise me.

MOLLY. He won't do silly paintings on the walls?

JIM. No, he's a potter. And this is the big news.

MOLLY. What?

JIM. Well, since I'm settling down, I thought I'd look for a place in the country. And I've found one, and I've made an offer.

MOLLY. Where?

JIM. In Norfolk.

MOLLY. It's a very big change. I oughtn't to ask you this, so don't be cross. But is it all right with that nice military man who we met in Fortnum's?

JIM (*annoyed*). Yes, Mother, it's fine!

(*As if to camera.*) Nothing knocks the glamour off being a sometime secret agent like one's MI6 Case Officer being on nodding terms with one's mother. Colonel Webb-Prosser was a dapperly suited, ex-Indian Army officer with a bachelor flat in Half Moon Street, to which he invited me twice a year to chat about cricket, coloured immigration and the state of West End theatre. And *nothing* else. My career as a spy has no function in this story, except as the cause of overheated speculation in others. As in Norfolk, for example, that first night.

The House in Norfolk

Unrenovated. It's dark. LOUIS *appears in the doorway, cheerful, with an armful of bedding and a lamp.*

LOUIS. Pillows, blankets, sleeping bag. I'll get the stuff from the trunk.

JIM. You need any help?

LOUIS. Yeah, light the lamp.

He goes out. JIM *spreads out sleeping bags and blankets on the floor. He lights the lamp and pumps it up. Thump of a car boot closing.* LOUIS *comes back with a box of DIY and decorating stuff.*

I brought a present for the house.

He produces the pot that was here at the start of the play.

It's a stoneware bowl, cut and planed. I used a warm grey glaze and a rust glaze. It's a subdued piece, because that's how I felt when I made it. I'm imprinted in it. Hold it.

He gives it to JIM.

Does it weigh more, or less, than you thought it would when you looked at it?

JIM. The same.

LOUIS. That's one of the signs of a good pot.

He takes it back. Looks round.

Where should it go? Yup.

He puts it somewhere prominent.

I've got the glasses, where's the whisky?

JIM. Here.

He gets out a bottle and pours for them both.

Let's go out early in the morning. Market towns are fun on Saturdays. We'll have sherry and bar snacks at some Betjemanesque hotel. Nice women in brogues with shopping

bags and wooffley dogs. We'll see that man about the
telephone line. Track down a builder.

LOUIS. That wall's gotta go.

JIM looks at it in some surprise.

JIM. Has it? Oh, all right.

LOUIS. And somebody, not the local builder, makes a beautiful
wooden spiral staircase up to the bedrooms.

JIM. Whatever you want. And then, on Sunday, let's just relax.
Dig up some brambles. Not get the papers. Fuck Ken Tynan.
Fuck Mary McCarthy.

LOUIS. Sounds good. You ready for bed?

*LOUIS takes off shoes and jacket and gets into bed. JIM
looks round.*

What?

JIM. Alarm clock.

LOUIS. The sun'll wake us.

He produces a canister of pills and takes one.

JIM. Are those mine?

LOUIS. Sure. I helped myself in the car.

JIM. What for?

LOUIS. I like them.

JIM. They're for sleeping.

LOUIS. They're even better if you stay awake. Didn't you know
that?

He laughs.

Come to bed.

JIM. I'll be back in a minute.

*He goes outside for a pee. LOUIS takes another pill. JIM
comes back.*

It's warm outside. Millions of stars and a full moon. I don't
think I've ever been so happy in my whole life.

He closes the door for the night and gets ready for bed.

LOUIS. Jim.

JIM. Mm hm?

LOUIS. Jim, we shouldn't get a phone line.

JIM. Why not?

LOUIS. If we've got a phone, then people can listen to what we say.

JIM. You don't mean, tap it?

LOUIS. Sure. Or use it as a highly sensitive bug, so it can reach into every room. They can do that.

JIM. Who can?

LOUIS. The people you work for.

JIM. In *Panorama*?

LOUIS. No, not fucking *Panorama*! I'm talking about your spy chiefs, Jim. Jesus! How naive can you be?

JIM. Just stop for a minute. This is all balls.

LOUIS. Is it? Haven't you noticed how strangely the phone behaves in London? It rings and there's no one there, or you make a call and there's a couple of clicks and an echo . . .

JIM. This is England. Primitive phones. Anyway, my so-called spy chiefs haven't got the faintest interest in me. I left when I joined the BBC.

LOUIS. I thought that nobody left.

JIM. You go dormant. I'm deeply dormant. I'm in permanent hibernation. Just drop it, will you?

LOUIS. OK.

Pause.

One question.

JIM. What?

LOUIS. Why did you go dormant?

JIM. I despised the work. It's futile. It's just lines of unattractive men fiddling with each other. It bears the same relation to international politics as cottaging does to sex.

LOUIS. Is that meant to be a joke?

JIM. Yes, it is. I think it's rather a good one. Spying's not a serious activity. It's a farce.

LOUIS. What about Suez?

JIM. That was in 1956, for God's sake. It's just a funny story I tell at dinner parties.

LOUIS. Tell it again.

JIM. I was in Cairo, and I was ordered to take fifty thousand dollars in cash to an Egyptian at the Mena House Hotel, only he never showed up.

LOUIS. What was the money for?

JIM. They didn't tell me.

LOUIS. Guess.

JIM. Well, I assumed that he was being paid to assassinate President Nasser. And yes, we can all be very shocked about it now, but the truth is that it would have saved a hell of a lot of trouble.

LOUIS. Why didn't the guy show up?

JIM. I've no idea. Maybe he got cold feet. Maybe they caught him and shot him.

LOUIS. Not so funny for him.

JIM. It goes with the job. And frankly, Louis, *if* MI6 is bugging the two of us, what the hell does it matter? I mean, what will they do? Expose me? And have another queer scandal on their hands? I don't think so. And your smoking the occasional joint isn't going to bother anyone.

LOUIS *takes a pill. He's in acute anxiety.*

Now what're you doing?

LOUIS. Jim, I'm frightened.

JIM. Why?

LOUIS. I shouldn't be here.

JIM. Where? In Norfolk? What're you talking about?

LOUIS. I ought to be in Toronto.

He cries. JIM *doesn't approach him*.

JIM. Why?

LOUIS. I'm still a patient there. I'm still on the list.

JIM. What about your certificate?

LOUIS. I made that up. I'm self-discharged.

JIM. You just walked out?

LOUIS. Sure. Through the doors, across the lawn and out the
gates, with bandages halfway up my arms. They could find
me at any time, Jim. They could take me back.

JIM. Well, what I suggest is that we behave as though it never
happened. I really don't think that there's some undercover
team looking out for escaped Canadian mental patients. Just
go easy on the pills, OK? I'm putting the lamp out.

He does.

LOUIS. Jim.

JIM. What?

LOUIS. How do I know you're dormant?

JIM. Because I've told you.

LOUIS. How do I know you're telling the truth?

JIM. I don't know. I don't want to talk about it, I'm too upset.
Pass me the pills.

LOUIS *does*. JIM *takes a pill and keeps the canister. After a
moment:*

I may be an arrogant, mean, cold-hearted cunt, but I do not
lie. Look at me. Can't you see that?

LOUIS. It's never you.

He sits up.

I thought you were only a fake in front of the camera. But you're always faking. When you're telling your half-ass stories, when you're typing out your shit, even now you're here. The only time I get to look in your eyes and know you're real, is when I'm fucking you.

JIM. I try.

LOUIS. Try harder.

Pause.

JIM. I can't stand this.

He collects some bedding.

LOUIS. What're you doing?

JIM. I'm going outside.

He goes out of the door into the . . .

Studio at Lime Grove

Anticipatory buzz. JOAN MARSDEN *is floor managing as always.* ROBIN *is there, checking his notes.* DANIEL *is on the fringes of the action.* JIM *approaches him.*

JIM. Will you hang on to these for me?

He takes out a packet of Senior Service and a lighter.

I'm told I mustn't have lumpy pockets. What's your name?

DANIEL. Daniel.

JIM. Would you stand where I can see you, Daniel? I'd appreciate having a human being to look at.

The Prime Minister, the Rt. Hon. HAROLD WILSON, *MP, is accompanied into the studio by* RAY RAY *and others.* WILSON *is smoking a cigar and is in perky raconteur mode.* ROBIN *moves over briskly to meet him.*

ROBIN. Good evening, Prime Minister.

WILSON. Hello there, Robin. What's this I hear? You're getting married? Who's the lucky lady?

ROBIN. As a matter of fact, Prime Minister, she's a very brilliant legal scholar at Oxford University.

WILSON. Well, that's one qualification for a wife, I suppose.

There's a ripple of laughter.

RAY RAY. Prime Minister, may I introduce James Mossman?

WILSON. Good to meet you, Jim. I've seen you often on the box. I was just telling your colleagues here a very interesting story about political bias. Well, *I* thought it was interesting.

RAY RAY. Oh, very much so.

WILSON *addresses them all.*

WILSON. I was in Bradford Town Hall last week, and I spied a young photographer jostling for my attention. I know him, of course. Amusing fellow, sells his stuff to *The Times*. He said to me, 'Prime Minister, would you be so good as to take a few steps to the left, where the light is better?' Of course, I've been in this game for quite a bit longer than he has, so I took the precaution of glancing round to see what kind of background he'd be giving me. Well, it appears that there's been an epidemic of petty theft in Bradford, so the Council had put up a poster of some sinister-looking individual, and up at the top, right over where my face would be, it said in big letters, 'Don't let him pick your pocket'!

Laughter.

There you have it. Bias all round. And then they say there's no conspiracy.

JOAN *is there.*

JOAN. We're ready for you now, Prime Minister.

WILSON. Somebody take this. Where do you want me, Mother?

DANIEL *takes his cigar.* WILSON *takes a pipe out of his pocket and quickly lights it. He,* ROBIN *and* JIM *move into place.*

JOAN. Just a dab of powder on the forehead, Prime Minister.

She applies it. ROBIN *produces his list of topics.*

ROBIN (*to* JIM). Jim, a minor change. I feel that I ought to lead with this.

He points to the top of the list: new figures on unemployment.

WILSON (*to* JOAN). Not too much. Just take the shine off.

JIM. Then what about industry?

ROBIN. It won't get lost. You can bring it in yourself as a follow-up. Then you lead on prices and incomes restraint, and we're back on track. The important thing is to stick to the eight main topics.

JOAN. Quiet in the studio, please. Clock running.

The clock runs 10 to 1. Film and music play. Lights turn from green to red. JOAN *signals to* ROBIN.

ROBIN (*to camera*). Good evening, and welcome to tonight's special edition of *Panorama*. James Mossman and I will be interviewing the Prime Minister, the Right Honourable Harold Wilson, on the issues of the day, starting with this morning's figures for unemployment in the North-East. Prime Minister, would you agree that these are very disturbing?

WILSON. I suspected that you might kick off with that one. It is sadly true that, in the present downturn of the economy, the problems of the North-East have been exposed. It's like rocks on the shore when the tide goes out and leaves them stranded on the beach . . .

JIM (*as if to camera*). It was those fucking rocks. I felt a tingle of irritation coursing through my body like a tropical virus. I controlled it.

ROBIN (*to* WILSON). But since you would doubtless take the credit for a healthy economy, should you not also take the blame for a sick one?

JIM (*as if to camera*). When my turn came round, I asked him about unemployment benefits. He jumped like a rabbit. His eyes went cold.

WILSON (*sharply, to* JIM). But we *are* compassionate. We are at one with the working people of this nation. That's what Labour is all about. Or didn't you know that?

JIM (*as if to camera*). I realised that everything I was trying
to hide was somehow transmitting itself. I couldn't stop it.
I didn't want to.

WILSON (*to* JIM). I'd even add that, as an MP with a northern
constituency, I don't need lectures on poverty from a London
journalist.

JIM (*as if to camera*). Then came the balance of payments.
Same syndrome. Then Rhodesia.

ROBIN (*to* WILSON). . . . which would suggest, Prime
Minister, if I may summarise your reply to Jim Mossman's
question, that you see majority rule as a desirable goal, but
not an immediate one. Is that correct?

JIM (*as if to camera*). Then the nuclear deterrent. Then détente.

The mood in the studio has changed. ROBIN *is tense,*
WILSON *is angry and on edge.* JIM *is coiled in his seat like
a cobra about to strike.*

ROBIN. . . . and our relations with the Soviet Union will be a
subject of debate for many years to come. Now let us turn to
Vietnam, where there are, at present, two hundred thousand
American troops on the ground, and an aerial campaign that
grows more lethal by the day. What, Prime Minister, can the
United Kingdom do, to help bring the conflict to a close?

WILSON. I'm very glad you asked me that, Robin. Her
Majesty's Government has proposed a number of peace
initiatives, which our American allies have accepted. Sadly,
North Vietnam has turned each one of them down. Now . . .

JIM *interrupts.*

JIM. Do you deplore the war?

WILSON. Yes, I do. I deplore all wars. They're horrible,
hateful . . .

JIM. Then why are we supporting the Americans?

WILSON. That's what I'm trying to tell you. We oppose the
advance of Communism wherever it encroaches upon the free
world. That's why we have a moral responsibility to support
the Americans in Vietnam. It's why we speak up for them on

the world stage, it's why we share certain facilities with them and it's why we maintain a robust military presence East of Suez.

JIM. Though not in Vietnam itself?

WILSON. Correct. However . . .

JIM. Do you have any plans to send British troops to Vietnam?

WILSON. No, we do not.

JIM. Because the Labour Party wouldn't stand for it?

WILSON. No, not at all. It's because our troops are not strategically required.

JIM. But as a show of support, they might be very welcome, isn't that so? Have the Americans not asked for British troops?

WILSON. We discuss these matters with them on a regular basis. You won't expect me to go into detail. And since you have raised the Labour Party as a spectre, let me say that I do not believe that any British prime minister, Labour or Tory, given that he was in his right mind, would send young men to die on the field of battle as a mere show of support. We can show our support in very much more constructive ways, for example by mediating between Washington, Moscow and Hanoi. Because, whatever one's moral concerns may be about this dreadful war, there won't be peace until there is agreement on all sides.

ROBIN. And the responses from Hanoi, as you have told us . . .

JIM. Can one postpone one's moral concerns? Aren't they something one ought to act on at once, whether or not the timing happens to be convenient?

WILSON. Well, without getting too high-flown about it, we wouldn't shorten the war by five minutes simply by dislocating from the Americans, if that's what you're trying to suggest.

ROBIN. Which brings us to last week's statement by the American Secretary of State . . .

JIM *interrupts*.

JIM. We'll come to that. May I suggest, Prime Minister, that in a war which is concerned purely with ideology and power . . .

WILSON. No, that's not right . . .

JIM. . . . may I suggest that our support for America isn't based on morality at all, but on expedience? You spoke earlier of an economic downturn. Wouldn't that downturn spiral into chaos if the Americans withdrew their support for the British economy? Don't we *have* to support them, whether we like it or not? Why can't you admit that?

WILSON. Because it isn't the case.

JIM. So your support is based on pure morality?

WILSON. Yes, it is.

JIM. And you expect us to believe that?

WILSON. You're not doubting my word, are you, Mr Mossman? Let me spell it out for you. What our support for America is based on, is our shared belief in free choice and democracy.

ROBIN. We must move on. It has been reported from Paris that . . .

JIM *interrupts with vehemence*.

JIM. But if one is burning to death under a layer of napalm, one's not going to be very happy about being told that it's all for the sake of free choice and democracy. Where do we stand in relation to the killing?

ROBIN. If I may . . .

WILSON. No, I'm happy to answer this. We are against the killing by both sides. But we won't get anywhere by saying one of the sides must stop the killing.

JIM. Why not?

WILSON. Because one side *will* stop the killing, and the other side will go on with it.

ROBIN. Thank you, Prime Minister. My next question is . . .

JIM. But isn't it morally more appropriate to deplore the killing on the side where you claim to have influence? That's if you *have* any influence? Or else to admit that you're supporting a war that you know to be immoral and foolish, out of sheer, abject subservience to the United States?

WILSON. That's a disgraceful allegation.

ROBIN *and* JIM *start talking at the same time. At some point,* ROBIN *holds up his pencil in schoolmasterly fashion, and* JIM *swipes it out of the way.*

ROBIN. Which brings us finally to . . .

JIM. Just one more question . . .

ROBIN. No, no more questions.

JIM. Just one more, and I have to insist on a straight answer . . .

ROBIN. I'm calling time on this.

JIM. . . . because the question that the viewers are surely asking is whether . . .

JOAN *signals 'wind up'.* ROBIN *steams in, full strength.*

ROBIN. If I may, I put the problem in a different way, Prime Minister? Would you suggest that the stability of Asia, or the world as a whole, would benefit if America were unilaterally to abandon South Vietnam to a Communist takeover?

WILSON. And leave millions of innocent people to an appalling fate? No, certainly not.

ROBIN (*to camera*). And on that note, I must conclude our *Panorama* special. Thank you, Prime Minister. I apologise if we got rather lively between us.

WILSON *replies with malice.*

WILSON. I thought I wouldn't mediate between the two of you.

Music and credits.

JOAN. Thank you, studio.

The studio relaxes.

ROBIN (*quietly*). Prime Minister, I can't say how . . .

WILSON. Don't worry, Robin. You can't knock spots off an old dog like me. Good try, Mr Mossman.

RAY RAY. Hospitality, Prime Minister?

WILSON. I thought you would never ask.

RAY RAY *leads the Prime Minister out, as:*

Herbert Morrison, who was no friend of mine, once made a very intelligent point about the power of television . . .

He has gone.

JIM. Great pity we had to stop.

ROBIN. Do you think so? Have you totally lost your mind? Do you know who you've just insulted, with your sanctimonious prattle about morality? It wasn't Chief Bongo Bongo of Chad. It was the Prime Minister of Great Britain and Northern Ireland.

JIM. He seemed perfectly happy.

ROBIN. Don't let that fool you. He's a snake. Number 10 will be screaming down the telephone in the morning, and the Director-General will be incandescent. He's got the licence fee coming up, for God's sake. *And* you knocked my pencil aside!

JIM. It was in my way!

ROBIN *goes.* DANIEL *is there with* JIM*'s cigarettes and lighter.*

DANIEL. I thought it was great.

JIM *nods absently. Takes the cigarettes.*

JIM (*as if to camera*). A summons arrived from Ray Ray. I felt my protective halo wearing thin. Was I about to be fired? I resolved to go down with all flags flying. In fact, I didn't go down at all, thanks to something I had forgotten in my years on the road: the BBC's long-practised skill at damage limitation.

Ray Ray's Office

RAY RAY *welcomes* JIM *in friendly and avuncular fashion.*

RAY RAY. Jim, come in.

JIM *does.*

JIM. Nice new office.

RAY RAY. Yes, isn't it? A decent view and I get an extra yard of carpet. It's a curious move. Not an ominous one. I've been assured of that. Do sit down.

JIM *does.*

I have been deemed the appropriate person to deal with the Mossman problem.

JIM. I still don't see that I did anything wrong. The PM lied.

RAY RAY. That's neither here nor there. They all lie. That man wouldn't know the truth if he discovered it in his morning egg. But there's a difference between forensic exposure and being bloody rude.

JIM. I wasn't much ruder than Cruel Glasses often is.

RAY RAY. Yes, you were. Anyway, Cruel Glasses can get away with it, and you can't. It's just one of those things. Don't make this difficult for me.

JIM. Why not?

RAY RAY. Because I've been working my socks off, trying to make it easy for *you*. Now, are you listening?

JIM. Yes.

RAY RAY. Good. Here's where we are. Number 10 wants your head on a platter, but the DG has made the firm decision not to give it to them, (a) because he knows your value to the Corporation. As we all do.

JIM. What's (b)?

RAY RAY. (b), as you very well know, is that if we buckle under over you, there'll be no stopping the blighters. The DG is, however, inclined to make a propitiatory gesture.

JIM. Such as what?

RAY RAY. You will be reprimanded.

He makes a note on a piece of paper.

JIM. Who's going to reprimand me?

RAY RAY. I am.

JIM. Then you'd better get on with it.

RAY RAY. I've done it.

He holds up the piece of paper.

There. I'm sure you'll stay out of trouble in future.

JIM. I can't guarantee that.

RAY RAY. Very funny.

JIM. Is that it?

RAY RAY. Not quite.

He takes a moment before continuing.

There is a feeling, Jim, that your talents are not being used to their best advantage.

JIM *senses the sack coming up.*

JIM. What's the problem?

RAY RAY. It's the studio. It seems to bring out something too contentious in you. It's no reflection on your skills. As a foreign reporter, you were A1. Total professional, commanding presence, very good walker . . .

JIM. *Walker?*

RAY RAY. Yes, walking's very important. One sees these people nowadays, marching up and down like robots, hands in the air, and as for walking and talking at the same time, forget it!

He laughs.

But you, whatever godforsaken outpost you were in, you always looked terrific.

JIM. Well, I'm very flattered, Ray Ray, but I do understand that the days of the patrician Englishman in a crumpled linen suit are probably over.

RAY RAY. That is the general feeling, yes.

JIM. So if I'm not on the road, and I'm not in the studio, what's left?

RAY RAY. Well, that's the puzzle. You see, we do have to find you *something*. We've taken that line.

JIM *decides to chance it*.

JIM. How would it be if I did some serious film-making?

RAY RAY. What kind of film-making?

JIM. Not snippets. Decent length. People, politics, state of the world.

RAY RAY. Go on.

JIM. I'd want to go for a different style.

RAY RAY. I'm listening.

JIM. More like life, as it really is.

RAY RAY. Can you tell me more?

JIM. Not off the cuff. I'd have thought that you knew me well enough by now to trust me.

RAY RAY. Indeed. No question about it. Just get something down on paper. You realise, don't you, that I can't give you a yea or nay? I'm not a controller, nor an editor. But I'll speak to the relevant people.

He stands.

JIM. Tell them that I don't want some prick of a producer breathing down my neck.

RAY RAY. A producer is mandatory nowadays. But if you make a recommendation, it will be considered.

JIM (*as if to camera*). It was 1968. In Prague, young people died defying the Russian tanks. In Paris, they tore up the streets to defy de Gaulle. In Washington, LBJ skulked like a criminal in the White House, defied by chants of accusation. Children defied their parents, scorched their brains with drugs, revelled in sex. It was at the height of the year's delirium that news of Death Number Three was conveyed obliquely to us in a dreary suburb of the city of love and

flowers: San Francisco. Ray Ray had talked to the relevant
people. We were filming.

San Francisco

LOUIS *and* DANIEL *are at the table in the dining room of a
suburban house.* LOUIS *is putting together a shooting schedule,
using lots of sheets of paper and different coloured pens.* JIM *is
drinking whisky and reading* No One Writes to the Colonel *by
Gabriel García Márquez.* LOUIS *takes a pill and looks round in
disgust.*

LOUIS. Look at this place. Plastic chairs. Wild West fireplace.
There isn't one thing in this house that isn't mass-produced.

DANIEL. You chose it.

LOUIS. Thank you, Daniel, for that unbelievably negative and
destructive comment.

DANIEL. I only . . .

LOUIS. Being the producer doesn't entitle you to interfere. Now
maybe you'll let me finish the shooting schedule.

DANIEL. Shouldn't I do that?

LOUIS. No, you'll just drag it down to the same old grey
plateau of BBC bureaucracy.

JIM. Give him a break.

LOUIS. Oh great! I'll stick to the clerical work!

The doorbell chimes: 'ding dong'.

JIM. Somebody answer that.

LOUIS. Better be me. I'm only the gofer. 'Ding dong'!

He goes.

JIM. You OK?

DANIEL. Sort of, yes. I just keep feeling that we should have
got to Los Angeles for the Primary.

JIM. There'd have been no point. It was obvious who was going to win. Wasn't it?

DANIEL. Yes, but . . .

JIM. Then that's all settled. And look, the, er, the thing about Louis . . .

DANIEL. No, it's . . .

JIM. I know it's difficult for you. But he's essential to the film. He's in tune with what it's about.

LOUIS *comes back in.*

LOUIS. I've worked out how we can show the kids. We have the little boy firing his toy gun around the yard, bang, bang, bang, while the camera goes pulsing backwards and forwards, cinéma-vérité style . . .

JIM. Just don't start telling Marko about cinéma-vérité. He's just had a horrible time with the Maysles brothers. Do it all through me.

LOUIS. So what am I doing here? Jesus!

He goes out.

JIM. We'll have to handle things rather carefully between those two. When they met in London, Marko got deeply embarrassing about our time in Vietnam, and Louis got paranoid.

DANIEL. Well, we don't want that. Oh, were you and Marko . . . ?

JIM. What? God, no! He's a monster with the women. But he . . .

MARKO *comes in, carrying his Arriflex.*

MARKO. Jim! Amazing!

He embraces JIM. LOUIS *comes back in.*

JIM. Good to see you, Marko.

MARKO. I love you, I love you. Louis, I didn't expect to find you here. You got free trip?

JIM. Louis is our researcher.

MARKO. Researcher, huh? Do you get screen credit, Louis?

LOUIS *is about to protest that he isn't.*

JIM. Let's not get into that. This is Daniel. He's our producer.

MARKO *shakes* DANIEL*'s hand.*

MARKO. How old are you?

DANIEL. Twenty-five.

MARKO. What you produced before?

DANIEL. This is my first film.

MARKO *laughs.*

MARKO. Good old Jim! (*To* DANIEL.) What are your interests?

DANIEL. My . . . ?

JIM. Tell him.

DANIEL. Samizdat fiction, free jazz and the New York art scene.

MARKO. Good. That's good. You know how I work? This is my Arriflex. That's it. No light meter. No lamps. I don't do none of that shit. No zooms. I *run.*

DANIEL. Jim told me.

MARKO. Did Jim ever tell you how he found me in Saigon? I was humping equipment for NBC. Did he tell you how he saved my life?

JIM. Shut up.

He hands a whisky to MARKO, *who takes a sip.*

MARKO. So Jim, I just checked in at your motel and met your sound man with funny name.

JIM. Super-Rat.

DANIEL. Because he's fast.

MARKO. BBC and fast? This I must see.

LOUIS. Can we all settle down and . . . ?

MARKO. Louis, I'm glad you spoke. I looked in living room just minute ago, and there is young woman in flowery housecoat watching TV with her husband.

LOUIS. They're the people we'll be filming.

MARKO. They told me. They want me to say to you, that you must sleep in little boy's room, and he go to sleep with them.

DANIEL. I thought that Louis was staying with us at the motel?

LOUIS. It doesn't matter.

DANIEL. I think it does. We're not guests here. We're using these people's house to film in. I think it's a terrible imposition to kick one of the kids out of his own bedroom.

LOUIS. They asked me to stay. Enough about that. Let's do some work.

They sit and settle.

MARKO. So what we making?

LOUIS. It's called . . .

MARKO. I'm asking Jim.

JIM. Two ninety-minute films, one here in San Francisco, one in London. The title is *Wars of Liberation*.

MARKO. So what we doing in Dullsville, USA?

LOUIS. Jesus Christ, Marko, why can't you *think* before you *shit* on something? Liberation isn't just riots and burning tanks. It's inside us. It's the naked flame that can either burn us up or free us. It terrifies us. But . . .

JIM holds up a hand to stop him.

JIM. Let me do this.

MARKO. So?

JIM thinks for a moment.

JIM. Louis's right. It's the struggle to free ourselves. We start here, in an ordinary American home, with a suburban family, who in normal times would simply go with the flow. But now they're slowly waking up to the issues around them.

Feminism. Racial inequality. Vietnam. We go to a Black Power meeting . . .

LOUIS. . . . Angela Davies . . .

JIM. . . . a political rally, a Native American enclave . . .

LOUIS. . . . but it's the family at the centre. These are the guilty clones who support oppression, sexual chauvinism, the war . . . you could draw a line from a burning village to this very house . . . I've got some good ideas for how to show that . . . but in the wife, there's an additional twist, because we see what she might have been. She's not some bigoted redneck. She's an intelligent woman who's been corrupted by her society.

MARKO. And she's your sister.

DANIEL. What?

MARKO. She said to me, 'Tell my brother he must sleep in Teddy's room.'

There's a moment of silence.

DANIEL. Jim?

JIM. What?

DANIEL. This isn't true, is it? We're not really making a film about Louis's sister?

LOUIS. Is something wrong?

DANIEL. Jim? Why didn't you tell me?

JIM. Tell you what? You knew that Louis was our researcher. This is what his research came up with.

DANIEL. But Jim . . . !

LOUIS. Why does he keep saying 'Jim'?

DANIEL. . . . I've just realised . . . she isn't even American. She's got a Canadian accent. I had a Canadian girlfriend once, and . . .

LOUIS. Tell the truth. You are disgusted because Jim and I are lovers.

DANIEL. I don't give a fuck what goes on between the two of you. I'm simply . . .

LOUIS. I'm bored with this. Sort it out between yourselves.

He goes out. JIM *opens his book to read.*

DANIEL. Jim, listen. I'm the one who's going to have to explain that we combed the United States for the ultimate filmable family and ended up with your boyfriend's sister . . .

MARKO. . . . who started the Vietnam War . . .

DANIEL. . . . only now she's having second thoughts about it. I mean, big deal.

MARKO. Whose film is it anyway, Jim? Yours or Louis's?

DANIEL *explodes.*

DANIEL. It's Louis's. Totally Louis's. Who's been popping pills ever since we left Heathrow, never made a film in his life and now it turns out that he's hopelessly overinvolved.

JIM. That's what I want, you twerp. Involvement. Who cares about objectivity? Can't we, for once in our lives, participate? These people matter to Louis. They're in his blood. They're what he escaped from.

LOUIS *comes back.*

LOUIS. I've been out of the room two minutes and already you're all talking about me. I don't wanna be here, but there's no place else to go. Those two have gone crazy out there. They're lying flat out on the carpet, they're in tears.

JIM. Why?

LOUIS. *Why? Why?*

DANIEL. Yes, *why?*

LOUIS. They were watching the TV, that's *why.* They saw what happened. *As* it happened. That's truth, Daniel! That's reality. It's not your BBC 'on the one hand this, on the other hand that' . . .

JIM. Calm down. What happened?

LOUIS. Bobby Kennedy just got shot. I think that proves my point.

He looks at them all with an air of triumphant finality.

DANIEL. What fucking point?

JIM. Be quiet. (*To* LOUIS.) Is he dead?

The telephone rings.

LOUIS. You bet he's dead. He's gotta be dead. He was walking through some hotel kitchen in LA and he got shot by an Arab. Why does nobody in my family answer their fucking calls?

JIM. Don't take it.

LOUIS *picks up the receiver.*

LOUIS. Hello? Hello? What do you want?

JIM. Don't say I'm here.

LOUIS (*to* JIM). It's Super-Rat.

JIM. What does he want?

LOUIS (*down phone*). What do you want, Super-Rat? (*He listens. To* JIM.) You had a call at the motel. Someone at the BBC.

JIM. Who?

LOUIS (*down phone*). What was he called?

Repeats as he hears:

'Dep . . . C . . . A . . . ' (*To* JIM.) Is this a person?

JIM. Yes, it's a person. Did Super-Rat give him this number?

LOUIS (*down phone*). Did you give him this number? (*Listens. To the others.*) Yep.

JIM. Damn. Tell Super-Rat thanks and we'll see him in the morning.

LOUIS (*down phone*). Thanks very much, we'll see you.

He rings off.

(*To* JIM.) Jim, why so stressed?

JIM. Why do you think they're trying to reach me? They've seen the news. They want to send us to LA to cover it. Marko, how long have we got you for?

DANIEL. He's here till tomorrow week.

MARKO. I can't postpone.

JIM. Then we've got to stay here. No one take any calls.

The telephone rings.

That's them.

They wait. DANIEL *moves to the telephone.*

Leave it!

The telephone continues to ring.

MARKO. Jim. We can be in LA tomorrow morning. I'll get unbelievable stuff. I'll get you city in shock. I'll get you death of liberal hopes. I'll get whole nation asking, JFK, Martin Luther King, Bobby Kennedy . . . where will this madness end?

JIM. I'm sorry, Marko. It would just be a story. This is real.

MARKO. You're crazy!

JIM (*as if to camera*). We stayed. Louis called the shots. Immense quantities of film were delivered to Lime Grove. Mysteriously, I found myself unable to write the voice-overs. For ten years, I'd been dashing them off in rackety cafés and jungles fetid with the stench of battle. Now the crossings-out piled up on the paper like a tangle of hairpins. Louis didn't mind. He didn't like voice-overs anyway. He thought they were Fascist.

A Corridor at Lime Grove

RAY RAY *appears.*

RAY RAY. Jim, can we talk?

JIM. Why, what's the matter?

RAY RAY. I've been racking my brains to reconcile the film that you proposed, with the one you've made.

A TEA LADY *appears with a trolley.*

TEA LADY. Tea, Mr Ray? Tea, Mr Mossman?

RAY RAY. Thank you. And a fig roll.

He takes them and pays. The TEA LADY *goes.*

JIM. Well? Have you seen it?

RAY RAY. Yes, I was called to see the rough cut. I must warn you, that the knives are out in a very big way. The kindest opinion I've heard so far, is that it's a promising student effort, marred by facile anti-American propaganda. Jim, I cannot afford this. I supported these films, entirely to help you out, and you've been putting people's backs up from day one. We had Robert Kennedy shot dead, people busting a gut to reach you, and you couldn't be found. Damned unprofessional. And then you cover the shooting with a boring suburban family sitting on a sofa *talking* about it. And now I hear that the woman is your researcher's sister. Can that be true?

JIM. It is.

RAY RAY. And he's your chum.

JIM. That's irrelevant.

RAY RAY. I wish it were. I cannot believe that a man of your intelligence . . .

JIM. Look, Ray Ray, I refuse to be bawled out in a fucking corridor. If you've got anything to say . . .

RAY RAY. No, this can't wait. Your film editor, first-rate man, unsung hero of public service, he's very unhappy. Apparently you and he have been cutting the film one way, and then your, your friend comes floating in, high on drugs and says it's, I quote, 'crap', and it all gets changed. Have you any idea of the damage this does to your standing in the Corporation? The next film's all set up, I suppose.

JIM. Yes, it is.

RAY RAY. Remind me.

JIM. 'Radical London.'

RAY RAY. Leave your researcher at home this time. I mean that.

He goes.

JIM (*as if to camera*). I did. Louis went crazy. The San
Francisco film went out as helpless cannon fodder against
some mighty salvo from ITV. The figures were minute. I still
couldn't write. Very extraordinarily, a bright red sofa arrived
at the flat. Louis had ordered it, in manic protest against his
own totalitarian rule of white and pine. It's that lurid, flushed,
incarnadine image, that I associate with the night that Daniel
and I returned from filming a play at the New Arts Lab. Its
title was *Vagina Rex and the Gas Oven.*

Jim's Flat

A red sofa. Night. JIM *and* DANIEL *have just come in,*
DANIEL *carrying some stuff from the filming.*

DANIEL. I'll see you in the morning.

JIM. Oh, stay for a drink.

DANIEL. Won't that piss off Louis?

JIM. No, he's in Norfolk. He's finishing off the house. Whisky
OK?

DANIEL. Yes, sure.

JIM *pours drinks. Unseen by him,* DANIEL *looks at some
sheets of A4 by the typewriter.*

I thought that play was rather good.

JIM. I didn't understand a word of it, but then I don't
understand vaginas either. Nice women. They're friends of
Louis's.

DANIEL. Is this the voice-over?

JIM. Don't read it. It's not finished. Here.

He takes the manuscripts and gives DANIEL *his whisky. Drinks his own.*

Television's a bugger, isn't it?

DANIEL. I love it.

JIM. What's to love?

DANIEL. I love it that everyone watches. So the programmes and the viewers are all mixed up. There are rich people watching *Coronation Street* and then, a couple of hours later, there are working-class families watching a couple of old philosophers talking about Wittgenstein. Not many, I know. But . . .

JIM *hears a noise.*

JIM. Hang on. I think there's someone in the flat.

He goes to a door and opens it. LOUIS *is there, looking sick and dishevelled. He's holding a canister of pills.*

LOUIS. I'm gonna die.

He collapses.

DANIEL. Oh, shit.

He struggles to get LOUIS *on to the sofa.*

JIM. It's those bloody pills.

He grabs the canister.

DANIEL. Has he taken them all?

JIM. I don't know.

He looks at the pills.

DANIEL. Jim, he's not breathing properly.

JIM (*counts*). Three, four . . .

DANIEL. Give me a hand. Jim!

They get LOUIS *on to the red sofa.*

We can't just leave him like this.

JIM. You're right. You're right. Where's my address book?

He looks in his address book.

DANIEL. Ring 999. Give me the phone, I'll do it.

JIM. No, I'm finding the number.

He goes on looking.

DANIEL. Dial 999!

JIM No, I don't want to do that. I'm getting Teddy Carpenter round.

He dials.

DANIEL. Your GP?

JIM. Yes!

DANIEL. Jim, are you sure about that? I mean, I just don't think that what Louis needs right now is a gay clap doctor.

JIM. We'll see what he says, OK?

DANIEL. No! Ring for an ambulance!

JIM. Ssh. (*Of the phone.*) No answer. He's probably in the bath. I'll try again in five minutes.

DANIEL. Bollocks to that. We've got to get him into a hospital.

JIM. You're right. We will. If that's what we absolutely have to do, we . . . Only let's not rush it. I mean, what's the story?

DANIEL. What?

JIM. Who am I? Am I his uncle? His 'room-mate'? They've got people in hospitals who ring the papers. How do you think the photographers know to be there, every time Judy Garland gets wheeled in for a stomach pump? Oh my God.

DANIEL. What?

JIM. What day is it?

DANIEL. Thursday.

JIM. Shit. It's Peggy Ashcroft's first night. Teddy won't be home till after the party.

DANIEL. So what do we do?

JIM. I don't know.

He pours himself another whisky.

(*As if to camera.*) I'd never advertised myself as a queer.
I would have thought it vulgar. But did anyone seriously
think that I was anything else? Yet, rather than be reduced to
one in print, I would have let him die.

Pause.

We waited.

They do.

DANIEL. He's moving.

LOUIS *opens his eyes. Shifts up slowly. Looks at them both.*

LOUIS. What did I do?

JIM. You passed out.

LOUIS. You filmed my friends tonight. I'm glad I wasn't there
to see you pour their beautiful spirit through your sieve of
mediocrity.

JIM. Take it easy.

Slowly, LOUIS *gets up.*

LOUIS. You had a chance, a tiny chance, to take back reality
from the people who control it. I gave you that chance. I
made you a beautiful film, and you're ashamed of it. What
fucking right have you got to show reality? You don't know
what it is. A kid throwing a Molotov cocktail through an
office window has got more right to be on TV than you do. A
housewife stealing a frozen chicken from the supermarket has
got more right.

JIM. Lie down.

LOUIS *picks up* JIM*'s notes.*

LOUIS. Oh, a voice-over. Terrific. Tell the peasants what they're
meant to be thinking.

He reads.

'Yet as the revolution destroys, devours, its enemies are
devoured, will its the revolution's, will the children be . . . '
You can't write. Stick to reporting. Why are you looking at
me like that?

JIM. I thought you were going to die.

LOUIS. I should die. You should film it. It would be your one and only work of art.

He goes out to the bedroom.

DANIEL. That is such crap.

JIM. He can hear you.

DANIEL. I don't care.

He talks more quietly, raging.

Go to any student bar and you'll hear some scrubby-bearded twat shooting his mouth off in exactly the same way. You only think it's interesting because you're forty.

JIM (*as if to camera*). The following Sunday, as in some inexorable cycle, Vietnam returned. A hundred thousand people attended an anti-war demonstration in Grosvenor Square. We filmed it all. Louis came for the ride. He was drunk all day. Stoned all day. We all had a late dinner in the Casserole in the Kings Road. Louis stormed off halfway through. I stayed till the end. Filming the following morning would be the work of an hour. Broken placards. Debris.

Jim's Flat

LOUIS *is lying on the red sofa, as before.* JIM *and* DANIEL *are there.* MARKO *comes in with his camera.*

MARKO. Morning, guys. Where's the coffee? You feeling better, Louis?

He goes towards the kitchen.

DANIEL. He's dead.

MARKO. Jesus.

DANIEL *goes out.*

Jim?

Pause.

JIM. I got home, and he'd passed out. My doctor said I shouldn't worry too much unless his breathing changed, so I went to bed. I came down later and he seemed OK. Then I came down again this morning.

DANIEL *comes back in with a sheet to cover* LOUIS.

DANIEL. Do you think it's all right to do this?

JIM. Nobody said not to.

He clears his throat.

I'd like you to get on the phone to Ray Ray and tell him what's happened. Can you do it from the bedroom?

DANIEL. Sure.

He goes out.

JIM (*as if to camera*). Was it on that crimson deathbed, that 'it' was born, bloodied and shrieking, on that Monday morning? Not entirely. Grief alone cannot account for 'it's insidious brand of poison. One must include the things that shame one. Complicity in a medium that demeans its subject. Professional failure. The looming approach of the Bayswater bedsit. Even the loss of my small talent for words might be included somewhere in the 'it'-portfolio. And what about guilt?

The Flat, as before

LOUIS*'s body has gone.* MARKO *has gone.* JIM *is there with* RAY RAY.

RAY RAY. What did you tell the police?

JIM. Just what Daniel told you.

RAY RAY. Jim, I'm so sorry.

Pause.

I hate to bother you with . . .

JIM. No, go ahead.

RAY RAY. Whatever I say to you now has been fully cleared
with the DG, by the way. The lawyers have been hard at
work, and the latest I've heard is that the inquest will be at
Westminster Coroner's Court tomorrow morning at ten.

JIM. Isn't that very soon?

RAY RAY. It is. They're good lawyers. *If* the press are there,
you will obviously ignore them. The rest of it's all very
simple. Just play a straight bat and tell the truth.

JIM. I hadn't intended to do anything else.

RAY RAY. Of course not. Jim, there are one or two aspects that
I'd very much like to . . .

JIM. Ask whatever you want.

RAY RAY. I gather that your friend's behaviour could be
unpredictable. Or do I do him an injustice?

JIM. No, it's true.

RAY RAY. Had he had psychiatric treatment?

JIM. Yes.

RAY RAY. But not in an institution?

JIM. Oh, yes.

RAY RAY. And what does your doctor think was the cause of
death?

JIM. Barbiturate poisoning.

RAY RAY. Do you know what these barbiturates were?

JIM. Tuinal pills.

RAY RAY. His own?

JIM. No, mine.

RAY RAY. Prescribed?

JIM. Yes.

RAY RAY. To help you deal with the stress of your work?

JIM. Yes.

RAY RAY. How did he come by them?

Pause.

The question could be asked, you see, whether you had provided these drugs to a mentally ill person, or whether he'd helped himself.

JIM. He helped himself.

RAY RAY. Without your knowledge? We can talk about that later. Had he ever mentioned suicide?

JIM. Yes, often.

RAY RAY. Had he attempted it?

JIM. Yes, many times.

RAY RAY. Do you know that?

JIM. Yes, I do. He had scars on his wrists.

RAY RAY. So to put it very succinctly, a talented but disturbed young man succeeded, after many attempts, in taking his own life. It's tragic, but it doesn't reflect on *you*.

JIM. It's not that easy. He had too many scars. It isn't difficult to kill yourself with a razor blade. You just get in the bath and do it.

RAY RAY. But he chose to take the pills.

JIM. Only a few. He left . . .

He looks around for the canister, then remembers.

They were seized by the police. He'd been taking them for months. Years. I could have stopped him, I suppose, but things were tricky enough without getting into that. They build up in the system. That's what my doctor says. They reach the danger-point and then you drink too much and bingo. It wasn't suicide. It was just a fuck-up.

He cries. RAY RAY *waits. When* JIM *has stopped crying:*

RAY RAY. It's in the nature of every tragedy to be ambiguous. But ambiguity is what we can't afford. It is essential, both for you and the Corporation, that you focus down these multiple contradictions into a single story that can be easily understood and soon forgotten. Now, I've told you the truth as it seems to me. But I can't instruct you. If the truth, for you, is a story of drink and shared medication and a troubled relationship with a younger man, then you must tell it like that.

JIM. I understand.

RAY RAY. So how did it happen? Don't answer at once. Take ten seconds.

JIM *waits*.

Well, Jim?

JIM. He killed himself.

(*As if to camera*.) Did I betray my lover? Yes, of course. But, by dying in such an idiotic manner, he had betrayed me too.

End of Act One.

ACT TWO

JIM (*as if to camera*). I knew I would kill myself. I didn't decide
on it. I discovered it halfway down a bottle of Teacher's on
the night of the inquest. I sat there, glass in hand, feeling that
I'd stumbled across an abyss that had always been there.
Thought about this. Crashed out. Woke up in bed next
morning. Sour taste at the back of my throat. Wet pillow.
Louis's half of the bed lay flat. Then I remembered why. I
looked at the clock and it wasn't the morning at all, it was
two a.m. I was neither drunk nor sober, just incredibly clear.
The method was obvious, pills of course. But could I bear to
hurt my mother? This question went unanswered as, week
after week, I got up in the dark, ambled through to the
bathroom, looked in the mirror, surprised, guilt-stricken almost,
still to be there, with only a hangover to show for my imminent
self-extinction. It seemed so feeble of me. I had survived
another day, not through anything even as grand as cowardice,
but because of a humdrum playing-along with normal life.
The BBC had shifted me over into Arts, where I could do no
damage. I didn't protest. I swallowed the humiliation and got
on with the work. I went to parties, where I talked and joked
through an invisible pane of glass, and people found me very
amusing. Having thought I would never have sex again,
I picked up a boy in the crush bar of the Royal Opera House
and, after that, it was chocks away. I did things that made
no sense at all in terms of a suicide plan, like renewing my
subscription to the London Library. If these were compromises,
what came next was utter capitulation. I opened a book in
Hatchards, and Death Number Five leapt out. On the island
of Bali, fourteen years before, a young woman had died of
polio. The book was written by her mother, a distinguished
novelist, now out of fashion. It was absurd. And yet it filled
me with a longing that I couldn't suppress. I met the writer in
her cavernous flat in Eaton Square.

Rosamond's Flat

ROSAMOND, *seventy years old, is the wreck of a once-great beauty. Flamboyantly dressed, with electric white hair.*

ROSAMOND. Mr Mossman? Rosamond Lehmann.

JIM. This is Daniel, my assistant.

ROSAMOND. Yes, we spoke on the telephone. Do sit down. Would you like sherry, Mr Mossman, or something more complex?

JIM. Sherry would be perfect.

ROSAMOND pours drinks for JIM *and herself.*

ROSAMOND. You were a travelling news reporter, were you not?

JIM. I was, for many years.

He laughs at the oddness of things.

Then the BBC had one of its periodic shake-ups and I ended up with my own Arts programme.

ROSAMOND. Yes, I saw your interview with Nadine Gordimer the other night. It can't have been easy to find much there. Can you choose the people you talk to, or are they thrust upon you?

JIM. I can invite whoever I want. My reason for taking up your time, is to ask whether you would consider giving me a short interview?

ROSAMOND. How short?

JIM. Fifteen minutes.

ROSAMOND explodes in incredulity.

ROSAMOND. What can one possibly say in fifteen minutes!

JIM. It's the most that anyone gets, I'm afraid. We'd talk for longer, and then I'd edit it down.

ROSAMOND. Well, beggars can't be choosers.

She gives JIM *his sherry and sits heavily.*

I'm surprised that you've thought of me at all. I'm very old hat these days. Most of my books aren't even in print. But . . . (*Annoyed at her forgetfulness.*) Did you say sherry, David?

DANIEL *jumps up*.

DANIEL. I'll do it.

ROSAMOND (*firmly*). Would you?

He pours himself a sherry.

(*To* JIM.) But I have made my mark. I was a feminist before feminism was invented. I proclaimed the power of women's sexuality when it was not an acceptable theme. I exposed the betrayals of intimate life, a phenomenon of which I have most ample experience. But that's enough about me. Which of my books have you been reading lately?

JIM. *The Swan in the Evening*.

ROSAMOND. I see.

Coldly, she puts down her glass.

Allow me to make clear to you, Mr Mossman, that if you wish to bring my earlier work, my fiction, to a wider and younger audience, then I shall be most interested. But if it is your intention, or the BBC's, to paint me as a crackpot, then I must ask you to leave.

JIM. Let me explain . . .

ROSAMOND. Let *me*. *The Swan in the Evening*, as you know, describes my daughter's crossing-over into the afterlife, and her living, I say her *living* existence there. That book has brought me more letters of gratitude from the general public than anything I have ever written. But the response in cultivated circles has been cruel and mocking. Some of my dearest friendships have been wrecked. I will no longer discuss that book except with those who have a proper respect for psychic matters.

JIM. But I do.

She looks at him, oddly perceptive and alert.

ROSAMOND. Have you some personal interest in bereavement?

JIM. I had a friend who died last year.

ROSAMOND. Not 'died'. Crossed over. Was this a special friend?

JIM. He was.

ROSAMOND. Did you grieve?

JIM. I think so.

ROSAMOND. But you're not certain?

JIM. No. I'm very unhappy, but then at other times I find I'm managing perfectly well without him, which is almost worse. He was a talented man, but very demanding, radical mood swings up and down the scale, and really the best solution for me would be if I could . . . (*He laughs awkwardly*.). . . forget all about him, but I can't.

ROSAMOND. Will you excuse me for one moment? I must seek advice.

She goes out.

DANIEL. This is all about Louis, isn't it?

JIM. No, it's not. I'm drawing her out. She's very impressive, don't you think? Like an enormous moth made out of marshmallow.

ROSAMOND *can be heard talking in the next room.*

ROSAMOND. But *should* I? I've only just met the man.

DANIEL. Listen.

ROSAMOND. Yes, I *thought* you'd say that, but I wanted to be quite sure.

JIM. She's on the phone.

DANIEL. She's not.

They listen.

ROSAMOND. You haven't mentioned that I've moved your picture.

DANIEL. She's talking to her daughter.

ROSAMOND. That sounds delightful. You must tell me all about it once they've gone.

DANIEL. Fucking hell.

JIM. She's coming back.

They wait. ROSAMOND *comes back.*

ROSAMOND. Sherry?

JIM. Thank you.

She pours him another sherry.

ROSAMOND. Fourteen years ago, I was visiting the little house that I had caused to be built on the Isle of Wight. I was kneeling down to measure the size of a floor, when I heard a knock, a bang, a rap. A blackbird had flown into one of the new French windows and broken its neck. I scooped it up, and felt an ominous thud against my heart. I went back in haste to the hotel, and found a message awaiting me from my son. My daughter, Sally, who was travelling with her young husband in Bali, had contracted polio and died. I took the train to London where the first thing I saw, as I came into this flat, was a letter from her, lying grotesquely on the doormat. I thought for a moment that some appalling mistake had been made. But it was all too true. I ripped opened the envelope and sat on the carpet, my suitcases beside me, devouring each last word. And whether what then took place was on the fifth or tenth or hundredth reading, I cannot tell you. I only know that I awoke from my trance of devastation to feel a light and warmth in the room that I couldn't account for. I looked back at her letter, and from her bold, familiar handwriting shone a new vitality. I knew her spirit was still alive. In the weeks that followed, her 'livingness' walked beside me like a twin. Now she and I are closer than ever.

She smiles and cries.

She has told me to trust you. She speaks to me every day. There is no death, Mr Mossman. There is only a transformation into a higher form.

There's a respectful pause while she wipes her eyes.

May I ask . . . what were the circumstances of your friend's crossing-over?

JIM. He took an overdose of sleeping pills.

ROSAMOND. Intentionally?

JIM. No, I don't think so.

ROSAMOND. Did he leave a note?

JIM. No.

ROSAMOND. Where was he found?

JIM. In the flat we shared.

ROSAMOND. Was he alone there?

JIM. No, I was asleep upstairs. It was just bad luck that I didn't get to him in time.

ROSAMOND. Of course, I see these things with the eye of a fiction writer. But it's a reliable guide. I feel you are right in thinking that your friend was the victim of accident. The determined suicide climbs up to his solitary crow's nest and then cuts the ladder, so that no one can save him. Do you wish to contact him?

JIM. No. I don't. With the greatest respect, I believe that death is the end.

ROSAMOND. Then why are you here? Not for your television programme. That's merely a smokescreen. Though a welcome one.

She gives him a card.

Take this. It is the card of a remarkable psychic guide, Mrs Rudge. She is a simple, uneducated woman but her gifts are great.

JIM *takes the card.*

And now, to work! We need to make a list of questions. David, would you be a dear boy and help me bring my books and diaries from the study?

She and DANIEL *go.*

JIM (*as if to camera*). I looked at the card, imagining myself
sharing a magnolia-painted waiting room with an assembly
of the sad and the second-rate, all living in hope, all seeking
comfort. I didn't want comfort. I wanted to die. I reminded
myself of that, and put the card in my pocket, intending to
throw it away the moment I got out into the street.

He pockets the card.

At home, I counted up my Tuinal pills like some Victorian
miser. Fifteen would do the trick, it appeared, plus plenty of
whisky and a doorstopper of white bread to keep it all down.
It was while gazing thoughtfully at my slice of toast in Lyons
Teashop, that I encountered a major setback. Having steeled
myself to write a voice-over for a fifteen-minute film about
Andy Warhol, I then polished it off without any effort at all.
I was stunned. It felt like old times. That night I dug out the
last of Louis's hashish and wrote the first two paragraphs of
something that was quite clearly a novel. The following
weekend, alone in Norfolk, I wrote the opening chapter of
a book that would take six months to finish, and another six
months to be published. What was I thinking of? Another
setback threatened a few months later.

Lime Grove Studio

*Transmission. Film is running. JIM is walking round, checking
his notes on a very small piece of paper that he holds in one
hand, where it can easily be concealed. On the monitors, a film
of a sculpture made of found objects. In the film, JIM is
interviewing the* SCULPTOR:

JIM. *And this was made out of objects that you found on your
walk from West Berlin to Hamburg?*

SCULPTOR. *But not just randomly. They are what I discovered
precisely at dawn, midday and sunset.*

JIM. *And how will the people who see the sculpture know that?*

The FLOOR MANAGER (*who isn't* JOAN) *calls, and* JIM
returns to his place.

FLOOR MANAGER. Ten seconds.

SCULPTOR. *That is not my concern. I make the thing itself. How people choose to interpret the thing, is up to them.*

End of film. Lights turn red. The FLOOR MANAGER *signals to* JIM.

JIM (*to camera*). Hans Roth's exhibition at the ICA continues until the end of the month. Next week, we meet the Italian director Luchino Visconti on the set of his latest film, *Death in Venice*. The novelist Rosamond Lehmann gives her first interview on television. And the photographer David Bailey introduces his new book, *Goodbye Baby and Amen*. Till then, this is James Mossman wishing you goodnight.

Music and credits. Lights turn green.

FLOOR MANAGER. Thank you, everyone.

As staff and crew disperse, ROBIN *appears.*

ROBIN. Hello, Jim.

JIM *is cool.*

JIM. Oh, hello Robin.

ROBIN. I was doing a spot in Studio B. Saw your name on the board. Do you fancy dinner? I'm meeting a couple of bright backbenchers at the Gay Hussar.

JIM. No, I don't think so.

ROBIN. Some other time, perhaps.

JIM. Some other time.

ROBIN *moves to go.*

ROBIN. Ray Ray sends you his best regards.

JIM. You've seen him?

ROBIN. Yes, I motored down to his place in Haslemere a couple of weekends ago. He's at a very loose end, poor chap. Bought me a ghastly lunch at his golf club.

JIM. Terrible thing, retirement.

ROBIN (*pointedly*). He has his pension. Jim, can we talk?

JIM. Now?

ROBIN. Why not?

He sits in an interviewing chair. Now or later, JIM *sits in the other.*

You've been very much missed in *Panorama*. Have you been watching the programme?

JIM. No, I've avoided it.

ROBIN. You know I'm anchoring now? Mother clearly thinks that I'm no substitute for Richard. Which I'm not and can't be. But my interviews have gone very well. Did you see me with Edward Heath the other night?

JIM. I missed it.

ROBIN. Shame about that. No, from a personal point of view I can't complain. But it's the programme, Jim. It's lost its way. The figures are through the floor. The trouble is, that the views of people like us, who know our stuff, who actually do the job, are being ignored. We're mere reporters. Powerless hacks. While any arrogant young whippersnapper can come down from Oxford or Cambridge and start making policy decisions. You and I used to jib at having producers. Well, now the producers have got producers, it's like a rabbit farm. Some little smartarse you don't know from Adam, comes slithering up to you and asks you what your 'line' will be on some national issue. I tell them, 'Watch the fucking screen and you'll find out.' Then they call me a prima donna. I don't care. Fuck them. I'm merely standing up for the robust individuality that the viewers have every right to expect.

JIM. I'm glad I'm out of it.

ROBIN. Oh, don't say that. There's a desperate need for a man of your weight. The new reporters are fine as far as they go, but they can't stand up to the smartarses. I'm fighting a solo battle. Would you consider coming back?

JIM laughs in surprise.

JIM. Me? Forget it.

ROBIN. Why?

JIM. They wouldn't have me. I was sent into exile.

ROBIN. Only to Arts. It's not Siberia. They had to do *something* after your, your personal difficulty. But that's all . . .

JIM. Dead and buried.

ROBIN. I wouldn't have said that. I would never say that.

JIM. I'm sorry.

ROBIN. I'm not being frivolous. I wouldn't approach you, if I hadn't first taken soundings.

JIM. Who from?

ROBIN. It doesn't matter. High enough. Come on, Jim . . .

He gestures around the studio.

. . . you don't really enjoy this nonsense, do you? You should be making your mark on the real world.

JIM. When did I ever do that?

ROBIN. Many times. Your first Vietnam film, for example.

JIM. That was the film that put me off reporting. It was inadequate. Worse than inadequate. It was an insult to the dead man.

ROBIN. Oh, what bilge. It woke people up to the war. A television report isn't a learned thesis. It's a story, and you told better stories than anyone. Don't tell me you don't miss it.

JIM. I do. But . . .

ROBIN. Well?

JIM. There's something else that I've been planning to do for quite some time.

ROBIN. Another commitment?

JIM. You could call it that.

ROBIN. Would it conflict with *Panorama*?

JIM. Yes, it would.

ROBIN. Are you quite sure? Could things not be arranged so that you were able to do both?

JIM *is amused*.

JIM. Not easily, no.

ROBIN. This other commitment *is* with the BBC, of course?

JIM. Well, no it isn't.

ROBIN. *Isn't* it? Did I hear you correctly? Are you seriously considering crossing over to the other side?

JIM. Yes, I am.

He laughs.

ROBIN. Jim, this is very grave news! Commercial television just isn't the same.

JIM *laughs immoderately*.

If you want a place at the top table of the nation, the BBC is the only place to be. You do know that, don't you?

JIM. I've always known it.

ROBIN. Then what's the problem?

JIM. Would I be allowed to make my own films?

ROBIN. Naturally.

JIM. What about interviews?

ROBIN. Why not?

JIM. I can't be tame.

ROBIN. Then don't be. You forget who you're talking to, Jim. I'm the Grand Inquisitor. I'm Cruel Glasses.

JIM. Then why was I banned from the studio after the Wilson interview?

ROBIN. That's a very good question. You were out of order. No doubt about that. Your reprimand was well-deserved. But for that single error of judgement to have such dreadful repercussions, has always puzzled me. You know that you were being considered for Richard's job?

JIM. No, I didn't know that.

ROBIN. Well, you were. Ray Ray was very upset when they ruled you out. That's all he'll tell me. But it seems to me now, that the key to it all is the look in the PM's eyes when you first spoke to him. It was a look of shock, of fear. I think he knew.

JIM. Knew what?

ROBIN. That you were a spook. Well, aren't you?

JIM. I was. What about it?

ROBIN. Wilson hated spooks. He had some mad idea that the Secret Services were planning to kick him out of office. Or was he right about that?

JIM. I haven't a clue. Go on.

ROBIN. Isn't it obvious? He thought that you were part of the plot. Hence the embargo on you. But now, with the change of government . . .

JIM. It wasn't that. I felt contempt for him. He saw it, and that's what shocked him. You don't feel contempt. That's why you're so successful. You think the politicians fear you. They love you. You bash them about the head for a couple of rounds, and they end up looking battered and bruised, but they haven't been hurt, not really. It's merely a show. And you and they are all in the show together. You're just the panto villain.

ROBIN. That's a 'no', I assume.

He gets up to go.

You haven't the right to feel contempt. They may be crooks. They may be charlatans. They may be brainless boobs. It doesn't matter. People voted for them. No one voted for us. Goodnight.

He goes.

JIM (*as if to camera*). A narrow escape. Thank God I burned my bridges. Very annoyingly, my grounds for despair continued to crumble. The BBC gave me a Christmas bonus of two hundred pounds for good performance. They said I'd shed the air of doom that had made my first series so painful to watch.

The novel flowed: Hong Kong, Saigon, the brothels, the bars. A foreign reporter, Cambridge graduate, co-opted by MI6, drinks too much and, just to make the disguise entirely opaque, a heterosexual. One autumn lunchtime in a cheap Greek restaurant, half my staff around the table, all young, all full of life, I realised that not once that day had I thought about Louis. I felt I'd lost him all over again. A few days later, I saw the psychic. It was a predictable waste of time. I swore I'd never go back. I did.

Mrs Rudge's Consulting Room

MRS RUDGE *is a stout, unpretentious woman.* JIM *is there, ill-at-ease. He has a weekend bag.*

MRS RUDGE. It's chilly this afternoon. Would you like me to turn the heating up?

JIM. Don't bother.

He sits.

MRS RUDGE. You've had a difficult week. All those artistic people that you've got to deal with.

JIM. Can we start?

MRS RUDGE. Whenever you like, dear. You're still hoping to hear from your friend, aren't you?

JIM. Or not.

MRS RUDGE. Well, let's see. Have you brought me something?

JIM. Yes, I have. It was in my place in the country, or I'd have brought it last week.

He looks in his weekend bag.

I know I packed it. Here.

He takes out LOUIS*'s pot.*

MRS RUDGE. Put it down. I'll see to it in a moment. There's too much going on.

JIM *puts it down. She continues in a matter-of-fact manner.*

Your dad's here. He's wearing his flying jacket. He's brought your Auntie Daisy with him. They're worried about your mum. They're saying her cough's no better.

JIM. You know that. It would be nice, just for once, if you told me something I hadn't already told you myself.

MRS RUDGE. You keep coming back, though, don't you? How many times is it now? Six, eight?

JIM. I don't know. People do all kind of things that they know they shouldn't. My mother smokes. It's an addiction.

MRS RUDGE. Why do you make everything so complicated? It's very simple, what I do. I see what's there. It's the gift that I was born with, so I use it, just like you do yours. Now you've confused me. Let's be quiet for a moment.

She closes her eyes briefly. Opens them.

That's better.

She picks up the pot.

Your friend made this, didn't he?

Pointedly, JIM *doesn't answer. She feels the pot.*

It's sad.

JIM (*witheringly*). The pot is sad.

MRS RUDGE. You know what I mean. It's quietly sad. I'm waiting.

Pause.

It can happen, when someone wants to hear from his lost and loved one, but he also doesn't, that the loved one will respect his doubts and leave him alone.

Pause.

Or the loved one might be so content on spirit-side, that the life he left behind has faded away for him. We should be happy for him then. It means that . . . Oh no, I'm wrong. There's a shadow.

JIM. Is it him?

MRS RUDGE. I don't know. I can't say more than I can see.

Pause.

Still just a shadow. He's holding back.

JIM. *He* is?

MRS RUDGE. Yes, it's him. Good-looking chap. Ssh. He's telling me something.

She listens. Quietly:

Oh.

She listens in growing distress. Glances at JIM, *then away.*

That's it. He's gone.

JIM. What did he say?

MRS RUDGE. He didn't say anything.

JIM. But you were listening.

MRS RUDGE. He said, this pot belongs in the house in the country.

JIM. I told you that.

MRS RUDGE. He says you're going there now.

JIM *glances at his weekend bag.*

JIM. Friday afternoon, weekend bag. Good thinking. Is there anything else?

MRS RUDGE *hands him the pot.*

MRS RUDGE. He wants you to take this back to the house. He says it's very important. There won't be anything more. I'm not going to charge you for this afternoon.

JIM. Oh no, that wouldn't be fair.

He writes a cheque. She takes it.

MRS RUDGE. Thank you. Have a nice weekend.

JIM. I will.

MRS RUDGE. You won't be alone.

JIM. Good guess. I'm taking a friend. (*As if to camera.*) I dismissed
   her melodramatic moment from my mind and drove to Norfolk,
   Daniel in the passenger seat, first guest since ever. Icy roads,
   sprinkle of snow, twilight evocative of dreams and partings.
   Outside the car, when I stopped for a pee, crisp air, sharp
   wind, hot steam from the frozen earth and a smell of stables.
   I see myself now, feet numb with cold, my back to the car,
   stock still, astonished by the realisation that had suddenly
   struck me. My quest for Louis had been rewarded with a
   message, not from him, of course not, no, it was all invented
   by that fraudulent cow. But it was true. His pot, so redolent
   of his moods, his subdued colours. Take it back to the house
   that we had made together. Love and respect it. Then leave
   it where it belongs and return to London. Leave grief behind.
   Leave Louis behind. I had mourned. I had recovered.

Norfolk

Wind. JIM *puts* LOUIS*'s pot where* LOUIS *first placed it. He
starts unpacking food.* DANIEL *comes down from upstairs. He
has a bottle of Glenfiddich and a briefcase.*

JIM. I hope your room won't be too cold.

DANIEL. I put the heater on. Oh, and I brought you this.

He gives JIM *the Glenfiddich.*

JIM. Thanks. Oh, very good.

He finds glasses and pours drinks. Meanwhile:

DANIEL. Great house.

JIM. It's all Louis. It was difficult coming here for a while. I'd
   bring in a log from the shed, and there'd be his axe marks on
   it. Or I'd see the circle of black on the grass where I burned
   his things. But then you get new logs and the grass grows
   back, if you'll forgive the clash of symbols. Here.

He gives DANIEL *a whisky, and goes on unpacking.*

DANIEL. Thanks.

JIM. Remind me about tomorrow?

DANIEL. We're meeting Rachel off the train in Thetford at twenty past ten.

JIM. She's the actress.

DANIEL. Yep.

JIM. Any good?

DANIEL. Oh yes, she's excellent. She's got that look that people like now, sort of skinny and wild but all the time you know there's a pony in the paddock somewhere. She's only playing a quayside tart in the film, but Tony Richardson's really excited about her. He's asked her to go to his place in the South of France when they've wrapped. I'm going as well, and what about you?

JIM. What, the three of us?

DANIEL. Yes.

JIM. To Tony's?

DANIEL. Yes.

JIM. No, I couldn't do that.

DANIEL. Why not?

JIM. God, no. Tyrannical party games, endless outdoor lunches, pretty boys splashing about in the pool, actually it sounds jolly nice, but if I'm anyone's guest, then I ought to be Tony's. Let's work, then eat. You were going to tell me your idea for the programme.

DANIEL. For me to direct?

JIM. Of course.

DANIEL *rummages in his briefcase, finding various papers. Meanwhile:*

DANIEL. It's a ten-minute film about poetry.

JIM. Modern?

DANIEL. Yep.

JIM. Auden, Larkin?

DANIEL. No, not exactly.

JIM. American?

DANIEL. No.

JIM. Then what?

DANIEL. I'll read you a bit.

He reads:

'When first we met, 'twas bliss to be alive
You were a girl and I was but a youth.
Now that the years have numbered twenty-five
How can I find the words to tell the truth?

He is reading from a colourful greeting card. JIM laughs.

'This silver wedding day for me means more
Than all the joys that time has swept away
For in that beauteous face that I adore
I see the history of each passing day.

'Ah, how can youthful loveliness compare . . . '

JIM. Stop it, for fuck's sake. It's unspeakable.

DANIEL. Jim, you think that, and I may think that, but who are
we to impose our taste on everyone else?

JIM. We're people who know about art. That isn't poetry.

DANIEL. But what is poetry? Do you know what Wordsworth
said? He said that poetry is 'an overflow of powerful
emotion' and, Jim, there are millions of people who think that
poems like this are *really* powerful, *really* emotional. It's
popular culture. It's reality. Isn't that what it's all about?
Remember in San Francisco, how we took those supposedly
boring people and we . . .

JIM. Daniel.

DANIEL. What?

JIM. That film was a disaster.

DANIEL. No, it wasn't. It was ahead of its time, that's all. I've got a mate who uses it to teach his students at film school. They think it's amazing.

JIM *takes a moment to absorb this.*

JIM. Why don't you tell me about the poems?

DANIEL *gets up and moves about in excitement.*

DANIEL. Right. We'll film some customers picking out cards in a corner shop and we'll ask them what they find so meaningful about them, and they'll tell us. Then we see the way they live. Which is incredibly normal, but with masses of interest. We find some old lady, say, who's got a new insight into her lonely life from a card that she got in the post. And then the Poet Laureate comes on and says, 'Yes, that's just what John Donne was trying to do in a different way,' and it's all very fast and imagistic, nimble camerawork, lively editing, actually using film as *film*. Come on, Jim, it can't always be you looking reverent in front of a blow-up of Samuel Beckett. So what do you think?

JIM. I think it would be the death of television as we know it.

DANIEL, *downcast, starts putting his papers back in his briefcase.*

DANIEL. Fine.

JIM. I mean, I like it. Make it.

DANIEL *is overjoyed.*

DANIEL. Really?

JIM. Yes. Just don't fuck it up, OK? I'll start dinner.

There's a loud bang from upstairs.

DANIEL. What's that?

JIM. It's only a shutter. Help yourself to the whisky.

He goes out. DANIEL *pours a drink.* JIM *calls from the kitchen:*

I've been thinking of getting a dog.

DANIEL. What kind of dog?

JIM. Not any kind, really. Just a cheerful black-and-white thing that jumps up and down going woof woof woof. I'd like that.

The telephone rings.

I'll take it. It's probably Rosamond.

He comes back in and answers the phone.

Hello? Oh hello, John. (*To* DANIEL.) My brother. (*To* JOHN.) When?

He listens.

What happened?

He listens.

I'll see you there. Thanks for calling.

He hangs up. To DANIEL:

I'm sorry. We'll have to go back to London. My mother's died. (*As if to camera.*) There were things in her flat that I'd known all my life. A silver napkin ring, dented with my brother's infant teethmarks. A button-hook, bitten by me. A decanter passed down by some mysterious branch of the family, supposedly titled, possibly Scottish, never met. Sheet music from a long-abandoned piano. A photograph of the father I hardly saw and can't remember, in his Tiger Moth. His sandalwood antelope from Cairo. His Royal Flying Corps medals, bedded in nests of purple velvet. His letters to her. His letters to me, complete with drawings of matchstick men and one of a sixpence. Her diary, which I felt shockingly free to read. 'Another boring day. Then Jimmy rang up, and his beautiful voice made it all seem worth it.' Press cuttings about myself, scalloped down the sides where she'd cut them out with nail scissors. Her ancient evening bag, her opal earrings and an empty atomiser still smelling of 'L'Air du Temps'. Her mother-of-pearl cigarette case. Her green-enamelled lighter. Somewhere around eleven o'clock in the morning, I stood with a doll's teapot in my hand, tears spouting from my eyes like those of a child in a picture book. And 'it' was there. It was there in the room. In me. 'You're free,' my mother had said to me once, meaning that I was not, that I could never escape. But now I could, and would.

I was pleased, a few days later, to get a telephone call from
Marko. He'd changed.

A Vietnamese Restaurant in London

MARKO *is there, calmer and less excitable than before.* JIM,
relaxed and cheerful, takes a seat.

MARKO. You know I settled in Rome now?

JIM. So I heard.

MARKO. My wife is Italian and my two daughters are as good
as Italian. I can work anywhere from there. I come often to
film in London.

JIM. Oh, yes?

MARKO. I tried to reach you every time.

JIM. I know, I'm sorry. I got very wrapped up in myself for a
while. I'm fine now.

MARKO. You look well.

JIM. I am.

MARKO *looks at the menu.*

(*As if to camera.*) It seemed important to clear the slate with
the people who loved me. And, mindful of Rosamond's
crow's-nest analogy, to fix a date when they would all be out
of the way.

MARKO. A Vietnamese restaurant in London must be
something new. I thought, for you and me, good place to
meet. You mind if I choose?

JIM. Go ahead.

MARKO (*to the* WAITER). We want rice-flour pancakes,
summer rolls and bun cha, all to share. And then pho bò with
all the extras on the side. Two beers.

WAITER. I bring you the beers right now.

The WAITER *goes.*

MARKO. OK?

JIM. Sounds good.

MARKO. Have you been back to Vietnam?

JIM. No, not for years.

MARKO. Nor me. To cover a war is a big adventure for a single guy, but for a family man, it's not responsible.

JIM. Sure.

The WAITER *brings their beers.*

MARKO. If it weren't for you, I would have been killed first time that we were there.

JIM. I doubt it.

MARKO. Why say that? I know you remember.

JIM. I do, but . . .

MARKO. We were soaking up to here.

He gestures chest-high.

My arms were aching from holding up my Arri out of paddy-field. I'd shit in my pants. Then we walked into village, and saw line of bodies under blankets, little feet sticking out in row. All government troops. The VC had taken their dead away with them, like always.

JIM. I know what you're leading up to, but it . . .

MARKO. We went into some hut and we found what they left behind. Helmets, uniform, small hole where VC tunnel opened up. Then suddenly, 'crump' and rush of wind and ground under our feet is shaking. It was M-79 grenade launcher. That Vietnamese Colonel who had done fuck-all through entire battle was bombarding village. Though VC had long ago fucked off into jungle.

JIM. OK, enough.

MARKO. I took my camera and tried to run outside, and you pulled me back. I went to punch you, and you pushed me into tunnel and you sat on my fucking head. I was so angry. Then another grenade outside. That one would have killed me.

Ever since then I felt great love for you. I don't know why you are always so English about it.

JIM. Because you make such a ridiculous deal out of the bloody thing. I couldn't afford to lose my cameraman, that's all.

MARKO. That's so pathetic.

JIM. We worked well together, we respected each other and we never lied. That isn't nothing, but it's not love. I don't love anyone.

They drink.

MARKO. If you never lied, what about that first morning in Saigon? Kim Philby had fled to Moscow, and you said it was nothing to do with you.

JIM. Didn't you believe me?

MARKO. No.

JIM. Quite right. But I couldn't explain it then. I shouldn't even now, only it's all such balls that I can't be bothered not to.

MARKO. So?

JIM. MI6 had posted Kim to Beirut when everyone in London, down to the doorman at the Reform Club, knew how dodgy he was. So there he sat for years, reading the traffic and passing it on to Moscow, just like he'd always done. Until a Russian arrived in the West with a lot of new stuff on him, and then the game was up. If Kim had come back to London after that, he'd have got forty years. That's when I met him.

MARKO. Were you sent to meet him?

JIM. People knew I was going there, put it like that. I found Kim waiting for me in the bar of the St Georges. He was sweaty and shaking. I thought at first it was the drink, but then, after a whisky or two, I realised that what was having this dreadful effect on him was me. I was putting the frighteners on him, just by being there. The next thing I heard, he'd gone.

MARKO. Was their plan, that you would get him back to London?

JIM. It's possible.

MARKO. Maybe your people didn't want him back. Maybe they didn't want a scandal and the CIA calling them fools for employing a Russian spy. Maybe they hoped that you would frighten him off to Moscow.

JIM. That's possible too. It's also possible that I made no difference at all. I just don't know.

The WAITER *arrives with starters.*

MARKO. You're telling truth?

JIM. Oh, sure. Spies never know what they're really up to. That's why every spy story ends with a question mark. Someone says to the spy, 'I know the truth about you,' and the spy says, 'Do you? Tell me, please! Put me out of my misery.'

He laughs and eats.

This is excellent.

MARKO. How would you like to spend a few days in Rome?

JIM. Would I have to tramp around a lot of old ruins?

MARKO. Do whatever you like. Stay in my house. Eat. Read. Play with the children.

JIM. I'd like to do all those things. When?

MARKO. Easter?

JIM *thinks for a moment.*

JIM. Easter would suit me very well.

MARKO. Fantastic.

JIM (*as if to camera*). The date was fixed. Easter. My next strategic journey was to the house that Rosamond had bought just over the Norfolk border. Alone in her garden, I saw the earth pulsating with new life. Tiny spears were poking up into the watery sunlight. If I hadn't already decided to avoid the futile joys of spring's effulgence, I would have made up my mind then.

The Garden of Rosamond's New House

JIM *is there.* ROSAMOND *appears as from the house, with a partially unwrapped package.*

ROSAMOND. I've found your book! It must have arrived during the week. My idiot woman had tidied it up. Oh, this is thrilling.

She unwraps a book. She reads the title.

Lifelines. An intriguing title. When does it come out?

JIM. Just after Easter.

ROSAMOND. Don't read the reviews.

JIM. I don't intend to.

ROSAMOND. Very sensible. Have you written in it?

She opens the book and reads:

Yes. 'To Rosamond. Love, Jim.' I'm very touched. I shan't look at it now. I have another empty day tomorrow, so I shall read it then.

She puts the book away.

What do you think of my little garden?

JIM. It's very promising.

ROSAMOND. The previous owners' taste is never one's own. I have my doubts about the summer. Too many hybrid teas. Take my arm.

He does and they walk a few steps.

I nearly slipped on the path this morning. It's no fun being old. How long did it take you to drive from Norfolk?

JIM. Half an hour.

ROSAMOND. Is that all? We'll soon be planning our diaries together.

JIM. Yes, I was thinking, since you're so near, that I could throw a little dinner party for you on Easter Sunday.

ROSAMOND. That would be marvellous!

JIM. No, but I can't, you see. I'll be editing in London all that weekend.

ROSAMOND. While I rattle around up here with no one to talk to.

JIM. Yes, I'm sorry.

ROSAMOND. I don't *have* to be here, of course.

JIM. I wondered about that. It even crossed my mind that I might invite a few people for dinner in London. Except that I can't, because my flat's so tiny.

ROSAMOND. Then they must come to Eaton Square! I'll get the big table out and, yes, I'll arrange it all. It'll be much better in London anyway, because . . . Now let me see.

She produces a small diary from her bag.

I thought so. Christopher Isherwood and Don Bachardy will be over from America, and I very much doubt that one could coax them into the countryside. Easter Sunday. That will be perfect. I'll write it down.

She writes in her diary.

JIM (*as if to camera*). It was done. It seemed too easy. I made a mental note to stuff her dinner party so full of famous people that my absence wouldn't spoil it for her.

ROSAMOND. I will admit to you now, that I've been not a little hurt by your elusiveness.

JIM. Darling, I rang you last week.

ROSAMOND. Yes, but it wasn't any good. You sounded rushed. I needed to ask your advice about a difficult letter that I've received.

She gets it out and looks at it.

It's from some women. The first paragraph is all about my interview.

JIM. Didn't they like it?

ROSAMOND. Of course they *liked* it. Everyone liked it. That isn't the point. They knew my work quite independently. It seems that they're starting up a new publishing house. They want to meet me for lunch at some new restaurant that I've never heard of, and they say . . .

She puts on her spectacles and reads:

'Each one . . . ', each one of my books, they mean, 'has timeless relevance to the concerns of women today. It is our sincere hope that you will allow us to republish them.'

JIM. That's wonderful.

ROSAMOND. Is it? I can't decide. I was worried at first that they might be screaming harridans. But I've read their letter through and through, and they seem very nice. But they're not established. But then, my present publisher is *very* established, and he's no more use than a sick headache.

JIM. You ought to meet them.

ROSAMOND. Well, I'll consider it.

She starts to put the letter back in her bag. Stops, still holding it.

JIM. What is it?

She looks up at him, emotional and in tears.

ROSAMOND. You can't imagine how awful it's been for me. To be forgotten. Out in the cold. Even this curious little doorway back to the world is a miracle for me. And it's you who dragged me out of the shadows. You changed my life. You know that I would have never have bought this house if it were not so near to yours?

JIM. I realised that.

ROSAMOND. When I look back at all the brilliant men whom I've encountered, there is not one who has been so . . .

JIM. Darling . . . ?

ROSAMOND. What?

JIM. I know.

ROSAMOND. Of course. (*After a moment*.) May I go on? Something very strange has happened. Since my interview, and all the attention I've received, my daughter's presence has become very much fainter. Can you explain this?

JIM. I could if you wanted me to.

ROSAMOND. Did I make a fool of myself over her?

JIM. You did rather.

ROSAMOND. I loved her, you see. All my life, whenever I've loved, I've made a fool of myself. There've been vertiginous falls on the kitchen flagstones, rifled dustbins, tears to drown the ocean and enough slammed doors to deafen a bombardier. I can't help it. Love, and the show of love, are indivisible for me.

JIM. That's what I like about you. We ought to make fools of ourselves over love more often. I only wish that I'd done it more than once.

She takes his hand.

ROSAMOND. There's no embarrassment, then, between us?

JIM. None.

ROSAMOND. Thank you, Jim.

With charm and dignity, she removes her hand.

JIM (*as if to camera*). It crossed my mind that, since making love with a woman of any description would be completely weird and counter-intuitive, why not with her? But the moment passed, and I returned to London where, in my short remaining time, I got the rest of the series safely in the can.

An Office in Kensington House

It is shared by JIM *and* DANIEL. DANIEL *is looking at a BBC memo.*

DANIEL. Somebody's booked us in to re-edit the Stuart Hampshire film this afternoon.

JIM. That was me. We've still got to get three minutes out of it.

DANIEL. What's the rush? It doesn't go out for ages. You know what it's like on the last day before the long weekend. Everyone's going to want to shoot off early.

JIM. Well, they can't.

DANIEL. OK.

He attends to his work for a moment.

About the weekend . . . ?

JIM. What?

DANIEL. Well, I don't quite know how to say this. Don Bachardy came to the wrap of Rachel's film.

JIM. Oh, yes?

DANIEL. She mentioned you, and he said that he and Christopher Isherwood were very much looking forward to meeting you at Rosamond Lehmann's on Sunday.

JIM. Oh no, that's all a mix-up. Rosamond's mad as a bird these days. Success has gone to her head. Did you read her profile in the *Sunday Times*?

DANIEL. But it isn't just that. Marko rang for you this morning. He asked me to tell you that he'll meet you off the plane at Fiumicino at eleven o'clock tomorrow morning.

JIM. What did you say to him?

DANIEL. I didn't say anything. I didn't know what to say. Just where are you actually spending the Easter weekend?

JIM. You know perfectly well. It's all arranged. I'm spending it with you and Rachel and the world and his wife at Tony Richardson's in the South of France. Marko's just being chaotic. I'll call him up and sort it all out. Christ, I nearly forgot.

He picks up a suitcase.

My luggage. Will you do me a big favour, and take it with you in the boot of your car tonight? It'll save me carting it about on the plane.

DANIEL (*quietly*). No problem.

JIM. And then I'll see you at Tony's tomorrow evening. I am so looking forward to this.

DANIEL. Good.

JIM. Don't look so glum.

DANIEL. I'm not.

JIM opens letters. DANIEL busies himself with his work for a moment.

I was going to tell you over the weekend. I've been offered a job.

JIM. What kind of job?

DANIEL. Current Affairs.

JIM. What as?

DANIEL. Reporter. Consumer interests, lifestyle choices. It's all pretty lightweight stuff.

JIM. Still, you'd be crazy not to take it. Is it because of the greeting-cards film?

DANIEL. Yes, it's so absurd. That was just a bit of fun that happened to take off.

JIM. Still, it did. I'm very pleased for you, Daniel. Thanks for telling me.

DANIEL. I'd never have made that film if it weren't for you.

JIM. I was doing my job.

DANIEL. No, that's not true. You pushed it through, when everyone thought it was going to be rubbish. And now you're letting me go without a whimper. You're the best person I've ever met, and I still don't understand you.

JIM. Does it matter?

DANIEL. I don't believe you're coming to France at all. What *are* you doing?

JIM. I've told you.

There's a long, difficult pause.

Look, can we stop all this, and turn our minds to the Stuart
Hampshire film?

(*As if to camera*.) We did the edit. I watched myself on the
flickering Steenbeck, asking the philosopher whether, if
someone was very unhappy, philosophy could be any help.
While I tapped my chest in blatant self-revelation. I thought,
'Well, *that's* got to go.' I left it in. I drove to Norfolk. Daniel
and his girlfriend drove to France. He hadn't noticed
anything at all.

Jim's House in Norfolk

Wind. JIM *looks at the sheet of paper in his typewriter.*

JIM. In fact, he had. He looked concerned, but I pretended not
to see. It's upsetting when people insist on caring about one.

*He takes the sheet of paper out of the typewriter, crumples it
up and throws it away. Looks at another. Reads:*

'I'm standing in the living room of a house in Norfolk.'
That's not true either. I'm upstairs, lying down in bed, my
breathing shallow, a blue-ish tinge at the tips of my fingers
and around my mouth.

He looks at more papers, then tears them up.

I had a quiet weekend. I read. I drank prodigiously and
ignored the phone. On Sunday morning I stayed in bed, half-
dreaming of a Shepperton film set, dry ice billowing, and a
plywood bridge perched over a river of scrunched-up foil and
dancing gobos. A bridge so slight and inconsequential that one
could cross it without even knowing that one had done so.
Except that once one got to the opposite bank, there would be
no 'it'. Got up, ate, drank. The sky got dark very quickly.

Looks at the suicide note and reads:

'I can't bear it any more, though I don't know what "it" is.'

Writing this note, I was struck by the firm sobriety of my
handwriting. It showed no emotion. I realised that I felt none.

He puts down the note and picks up LOUIS's *pot.*

Quite drunk by now, I placed Louis's pot nearby, in reference to the toxic mix of love and betrayal and loss that I'd discovered on the night of the inquest. I thought I'd got over all that. But what else could explain what I was about to do? I went up to my bedroom. Did as I'd planned. Lay down.

He runs his hands sensitively over the pot, as though playing a musical instrument. A shutter bangs upstairs.

Hello?

LOUIS *appears. He's pleasant and relaxed.*

LOUIS. Hi, Jim.

JIM. I thought it was you. How am I doing up there?

LOUIS. Not great. Did you find out what 'it' was?

JIM. No. (*He laughs.*) I had a good look, but nothing. It makes bugger-all sense. My life is good! That film that we made turns out to be a classic documentary. Working in Arts is fun. Current Affairs have forgiven me, and who cares anyway? I don't even care about bad television. Just how responsible can one really be, for the moral and intellectual purity of a blunt instrument? Are you still there?

LOUIS. Sure.

JIM. My mother died.

LOUIS. Grow up about that.

JIM. I did. I have. And I've finished a book, not a wonderful book, but a book. My book. I can look at it on the shelf and think, 'I wrote that.' So why am I killing myself? Is it because of you?

LOUIS. Nope.

JIM. Then why?

LOUIS. Because of you.

JIM. I can't accept that. It's so bloody unfair.

LOUIS. You're right. It is.

JIM. What now?

LOUIS. Wind up.

JIM. I've got nothing to say.

LOUIS. Keep it ambiguous.

JIM. OK.

> LOUIS *settles to watch.*

> (*As if to camera.*) The search has been abandoned. 'It' will retain its secrets for another day, another place, another victim. Was this just another spy story, one where layer after layer is stripped away in search of the truth, only to reveal a question that can never be answered?

LOUIS. Ten seconds.

JIM. Or are the layers the true reality? Is the centre empty? Is the story all there is?

> *He looks up at* LOUIS.

> How was that?

LOUIS. Good timing.

JIM. It comes with practice. Go on. I'll follow.

> LOUIS *goes.* JIM *picks up some notes.*

> (*As if to camera.*) By noon tomorrow, all these papers will have gone. The firm will send a car, or make a call to the local police. Every typescript, every notebook, every diary, will be driven away, tied up and archived in an office near St James's Park. There will be nothing left.

> *He props his suicide note against the typewriter.*

> Except for this. Goodnight.

> *End of play.*